100 Rules for Entrepreneurs

Real-life business lessons

by Neil Lewis

HARRIMAN HOUSE LTD

3A Penns Road
Petersfield
Hampshire
GU32 2EW
GREAT BRITAIN

Tel: +44 (0)1730 233870
Fax: +44 (0)1730 233880
Email: enquiries@harriman-house.com
Website: www.harriman-house.com

First published in Great Britain in 2010
Copyright © Neil Lewis 2010

The right of Neil Lewis to be identified as Author has been asserted in
accordance with the Copyright, Design and Patents Act 1988.

ISBN: 978-0857190-27-7

British Library Cataloguing in Publication Data
A CIP catalogue record for this book can be obtained from the British Library.

Printed and bound in Great Britain by CPI Antony Rowe, Chippenham.

No responsibility for loss occasioned to any person or corporate body acting
or refraining to act as a result of reading material in this book can be
accepted by the Publisher or by the Author.

Get updates and regular newsletters at **www.RagstoWreckages.com**

To all entrepreneurs who dare to think differently but especially those who take the knocks, learn the lessons and then decide to get up, get going and make it happen.

Contents

About the Author

Neil Lewis is a media entrepreneur and business leader based in the North West of England. A partner in MediaModo and the driving force behind new digital magazines, business events and entrepreneur accreditation assessments, Neil has over 22 years' experience in publishing and business investment.

His specialist skills include business strategy, online publishing and media plus business investment and start-ups.

Neil regularly speaks at university and entrepreneurial networking events where he shares what he has learnt from his experiences. MediaModo recently won a North West Development Agency grant to develop a new entrepreneurial accreditation scheme that will revolutionise the way that investors and entrepreneurs work together.

Acknowledgements

I want to thank the publishing team at Harriman House who stood their ground and forced this book to be better than I could ever have made it. Also, thanks to my family, friends and associates, who have stood by my crazy ideas, shared the successes, put up with the disappointments and have been there to encourage me when I needed it most. Lastly, thanks are due to my neighbour who kept me awake late at night and so gave me the motivation to write this book.

Introduction:
15 Principles of Successful Entrepreneurs

All great achievements in business and life are built on a willingness to stick to first principles – what you know is right, even though many people around you will tell you to do otherwise.

In this book I lay out what have become for me the 100 most important rules for entrepreneurs. They have been established through practice, refined through failure and proven under pressure – and all stem from a few bedrock principles that I have learned and carried with me through many years in business. If the rules that follow are the individual tactics of successful entrepreneurialism, these principles represent the overarching strategies behind them.

1. **Debt is like a disease** – managing debt and repayments slowly eats you up, and burns up time. Avoid it in your enterprise at all costs, unless you can't, in which case, take on amounts so large that it becomes someone else's illness. (Trust me – Rule 93 explains it.)

2. **Prove your business before you take on equity partners** – if at all. And proof means one happy customer who delivers an operating profit and is willing to recommend you to another potential customer. This simple foundation is the first base for any prospective entrepreneur.

3. **Leverage a good idea with talent, but without building liabilities.** This means that in the UK and Europe you must use freelance and contract talent and ensure you don't accumulate long-term liabilities for redundancy, pensions or other entitlements.

4. **Hire or contract with all talent on a local basis.** Yes, they can work from home or in their own agency, but they must be

within easy travelling distance of a single meeting point. This allows you to bring different people together with different talents to seek and find solutions to the inevitable problems that will crop up.

5. **Talent is defined as anyone who can take your idea and make it better than you can.** If you find you are giving a job or delegating the work to someone who does it worse than you would, then you have the wrong person. On the other hand, if you give the brief to someone else and the idea or implementation gets better, then you have talent. Do not compromise on this.

6. **Never hire new staff to meet growth** – instead you should have your team prepared and ready for action before you take on the additional business. Otherwise, you will hire in desperation – 'anyone who can do the job' – but you'll fail to get the right people.

7. **Business is not about jobs or 'saving jobs'** – it's about profit and then the talent you can engage with that profit.

8. **In fact, business is not about profit, it is all about profit margin** – as profit margin is the true defence for any business which hits a difficult patch. No amount of cash reserve can save a business if the profit margin evaporates.

9. **Learn to negotiate** – and learn to negotiate win/win meaning, simply, that both you and your negotiating partner do well out of the deal. That way you will build long-term good will with all of the stakeholders (staff, suppliers, customers and shareholders) and the relationship will develop new ideas and ways to earn a profit for all.

10. **Look after yourself** – without you, the business is nothing. So, preserve that most essential element – you.

11. **If you don't love your business, move on** – if you have built a successful business but don't enjoy it anymore, then move

on, sell up, get out. As a demotivated leader your business isn't going to last anyway, so sell it fast and find something new to do.

12. **Grow your business smart** – set a target of the annual revenue per employee or effective employee (regular freelancers count in proportion to their time) at, say, £100k per person and ensure that you constantly increase this as your gross revenue grows. This way, you'll become a smarter and leaner core team. If you fail to do this, then the business risks becoming Big But Dumb.

13. **Manage your managers.** You need a mechanism to decide whether your managers are performing – which you will need once your business grows beyond a certain size. The best mechanism to use is the team member or staff appraisal method. Note, this appraisal should apply to all your team – freelance, contractors, agencies and full-time employees (if you have any). And your managers' ability to spot weaknesses and act on them as a result of this ongoing appraisal process is the best mechanism for assessing your managers' skill. So use it.

14. **Avoid dangerous goals** – don't set a rigid target to sell your business for x million pounds or dollars within three years – it will only lead you to overwork a poor business idea and/or make bad decisions. Aim instead to build a great business that you love to work for and which has a sustainable cash flow and profit. That way, someone will come and buy your business for a large amount of money one day.

15. **You must build a strong brand** – all your ability to maintain price margin, and therefore profit margin, will come down to the strength of your brand – because anything you do can be copied, except your brand. I've put this last in the list, so you can put it at the top of your things to do.

These principles are in effect a summary of the 100 rules that make up this book – wisdom gained from years of starting and running businesses in good years, when everything was going well, and in the bad years when everything, and everyone, seemed to have turned against us.

The rules themselves that follow show how to implement these principles in a practical everyday way. Taking inspiration from them should allow you to learn from mistakes without having to incur the pain of committing too many of them, and to build on success by following what has, after much effort, been found to work – and work well.

Neil Lewis
Cheshire, 2010

The Rules

1.

Just do it...

The classic saying adapted from Lord Tennyson's *In Memoriam*, 'it is better to have tried and failed than to have never tried,' is well known. But, does it apply to entrepreneurs? Well, yes, only more so.

Reading this book, you will either be an entrepreneur or would-be entrepreneur ready to start out on your own voyage of discovery and possible riches. If you are an entrepreneur, one who has had to battle through the past few years (or many years) and is already battle weary and wondering whether to continue with your current venture or life as an entrepreneur.

Equally, you might be a wised-up entrepreneur who really has been there before, and has the scars of the failures and memories of the successes, and is just looking, as ever, to clarify and develop your understanding of your role in business.

Among business angel and start-up investors it is a generally agreed principle that they are better off backing an entrepreneur who has failed and is willing to get up and try again than either a newbie entrepreneur and/or, perhaps worst of all, an entrepreneur who is yet to make or maybe realise their first mistakes.

In my ten years of creating and building a growth company, I learned more in the last two years than in the first eight. My first business grew from a £2k investment in a London back-bedroom, with two partners, in 1999, to a £12m valuation and three partners in 2007.

However, despite the excitement and massive learning curve that we all enjoyed in the first eight years of growth, it was in the last two years of decline and subsequent closure that I really learnt my entrepreneurial lessons.

By August 2009 we took the decision to close the business, sell the assets and share out what remained. We walked away with nothing.

Was it a waste of time?

Absolutely not.

What I discovered – mainly, indeed, by making mistakes, along with getting some things right – was of incalculable value.

And so our first rule starts with **Just do it** – because there is no substitute for putting down the business plan and just getting going… and no better way of learning.

2.

Learn from your mistakes

Booms are not always a good thing.

If you are successful as an entrepreneur in a boom time then it can be difficult to say how or why that success came about – with everyone being lifted up on a rising tide, the quality of the boat and the seamanship don't always seem to come into it.

In a boom all sorts of soft business models get funding and grow – and some are sold on to suckers who buy the story too – and everyone appears, generally, as successful as everyone else.

And of course, in the narrowest sense – buy low and sell high before the market busts – some are successful without being, strictly, successful. It is this that makes some entrepreneurs wake up with a cold sweat wondering, can I do it again?

In fact, this is a problem for any successful entrepreneur who has never experienced failure. Can they do it again? Did the only-ever-successful entrepreneur achieve that success because they were lucky or because they were omnipotent?

And indeed, many entrepreneurs who have been successful – without failure, or perhaps not enough tough lessons along the way – have a tendency to believe that they truly are great and cannot fail. But they can.

Look at what happened to these highly successful entrepreneurs, who perhaps enjoyed too much success – Robert Maxwell. who over-extended his publishing empire and resorted to taking from his pension funds to keep it afloat, or Ted Turner of Warner, and his disastrous decision to buy AOL, which lost him US$8bn.

So, if you hit turbulence and failure early on in your entrepreneurial journey, consider it a gift. And one from which you can cement your humbleness and willingness to listen to others, yet at the same time retain a steely determination to make it happen, no matter what!

It is the error and the painful process of correction that teaches us that we are not King Midas – not everything we touch will turn to gold. It is so much better that way.

The errors in our own history make us open to new ideas, open to unusual ways of doing things…and yet…at the same time, stubborn and unyielding on those issues that really, truly count.

3.

Never blame the market

Some people take the view that businesses that fail in a harsh climate fail *because* of the climate.

I disagree.

Businesses that fail in these conditions, like my first business, still fail for the same reason – mistakes made in the past catch up with the business and overwhelm it.

The harsh market conditions – or perhaps the abruptness of the change – have simply served to bring those errors into focus. The fact that those errors were made in the first place remains the responsibility of the original entrepreneur.

The entrepreneur gets to decide who succeeds them, or if they give shares away (and to whom and on what conditions). If the conditions they put in place lead to the appointment of a weak CEO that destroys the company, the fault still lies with the entrepreneur: He or she once had the power to prevent it. If a line manager or profit and loss (P&L) manager messes up and brings down the company, then it remains your fault for hiring them or giving them authority or powers they were not able to exercise effectively.

You can't escape and blame the market or anything or anyone else for that matter: You are at the end of the error trail of responsibility. This is actually a good thing: You have more control over your success than you think.

Never blaming the market goes hand in hand with the very essence of being an entrepreneur: paving your own way, driving your own success, building your own great business. So don't fall for the excuse.

4.

Take care of yourself

If you can't get rich right now, concentrate on getting fit and healthy.

Your business begins with you and will end – hopefully with a successful sale, or acclaimed retirement – with you. You are effectively the captain of a ship. You must decide where you will sail, how to sail and who exactly you want on board.

And, if the boat begins to sink, you will almost certainly be the last to leave.

Staff and team members, like hands on deck, may come and go. You will get supplied from various ports, but it will always be your ship, and, as such, you need to take care of yourself in order to be able to take care of the business (or boat) and so get your crew safely home again, hopefully arriving better for the experience.

You have to hold it together and you must look after yourself, even if your business takes a sharp downturn. Even if creditors are pounding at the door, keep exercising regularly – you'll need this to get rid of the stress.

I've learned that the best advice for entrepreneurs is given out every time you catch a flight. The steward on the aircraft will always tell you: "In case of loss of oxygen, put your own mask on first, and only then assist those next to you who may have trouble doing so."

Looking after yourself is not selfish, as many people wrongly think; it is the best way to look after the people around you. If you aren't on your game, you will only let others down.

5.

Know yourself

Knowing yourself could be a whole book in itself. But here I have a very particular meaning in mind. For instance:

- If you find failure or disappointment hard to deal with, then you need to be aware of this and have a plan on how you will cope with the inevitable setbacks and delays that you will experience.

- If you are easily distracted, then find a way to balance this by becoming meticulous in setting goals and reviewing those goals to ensure you are on track.

- If you enjoy some things but not others, then learn to find people who are good at (and enjoy) the things you don't enjoy (and probably aren't very good at either).

In all cases, knowing whether you are a natural business sprinter (i.e. lots of quick energy early on but fade quickly) or a business marathon runner (steady approach which gets there in the end), will help you manage your own expectations.

In fact, probably the biggest challenge we face is managing our own expectations and that is why it is important to know yourself – both so that you can set attainable and inspiring goals, and take practical steps to accomplish them.

Know your weaknesses

Many entrepreneurs are not able or not willing (some are neither) to make the shift from 'doer' to delegator and hence in the early days of an enterprise there won't be enough delegation. At some point, the entrepreneur will realise this – usually when working nine days a week – and then begin an urgent hunt for a professional/hardnosed CEO or General Manager.

Recruiting the right management is critical to growing a business, and without it the enterprise will remain a wonderful, but permanently single-person consultancy. However, recruiting senior management into your business is extremely difficult and highly risky.

If you recognise that recruiting such management is not a skill that you possess or perhaps wish to learn (for none of us are born with it) then your solution is to sell your ideas early – once you have proven the basic concept. So, after the first phase of creating the idea and proving it with a pilot, your next step is to become either an excellent recruiter of talent or a great seller of fledgling businesses.

Now, you may be tempted to sell a fledgling business – until I tell you that you will sell it for thousands of pounds instead of millions. But selling early might still be the right decision. Never let greed push you further into the business's growth than you can go, or know you can go after some honest reflection on your strengths, preferences and weaknesses. Make the decision not on the money on the table (or lack of it) but based on your knowledge of what you are good at (and conversely, not so good at).

Even if you continue, don't forget that the time to get out is when you are no longer playing to your strengths. Hence, the timing of your exit is always about when you reach the limit of your strengths and not about a fixed goal or whether the market is offering you maximum value.

Know your personal management potential

Many entrepreneurs don't make great managers. There is no shame in admitting that. It simply means that you have to get the right managers onboard earlier or hand over control to a new owner sooner.

Getting the right perspective on your own management skills is a tough call for anyone. When it's your business, your idea and your baby, then it is even harder. Just be aware that you might struggle with this issue – so start asking yourself what you can do sooner and be prepared to act swiftly when it becomes clear what action should be taken.

Remember – build teams. The implementation of good management is all about the people that you put together and, don't forget, *how* you put them together.

You may have the best people, but put them in the wrong roles and give them the wrong incentives and you'll have a bust business in no time.

The building of a team is also a gradual process; you'll get it right sometimes and sometimes you'll get it wrong. So, make sure you hire people on a freelance or contract basis and not on a long-term employment contract. That way, if you realise that you've made a mistake then it won't cost you a fortune to change.

Know your strengths

There will be something at which you are uniquely qualified to do. For some people it will be sales. For others, it will be negotiating complex deals. Some entrepreneurs have a knack for trading – buying low and selling high. My special skills are in editorial and digital publishing.

All of us, I believe, have special skills. They might be quite specific skills, quite unique, but nevertheless they are something that each one of us possesses or has the potential to develop, and that very few other people have in the same configuration, allied to the same passions or together in the same time and place.

Therefore, if you know your skills, and can create a business based on them or built around them, you will more than likely be able to create a successful enterprise no matter the economic environment you find yourself in. A unique skill set, expressed uniquely, is a valuable commodity.

So, what are you uniquely qualified to do?

If you don't know the answer to this – or are not sure – then the best thing to do is to focus on what you enjoy most and find a hard-headed way to make it a business (other Rules in this book will, of course, help you there). You may change your mind about what your true strengths are along the way, but at least you'll enjoy it, and there is a reasonable chance that what you enjoy most is also what you will be best at.

6.

Measure success properly

How are you doing on your entrepreneurial journey? Good, bad, not sure?

You probably wonder what you might measure yourself against.

Some famous entrepreneurs such as Donald Trump have said about money that it "was never a big motivation…except as a way to keep score". If Mr Trump's view was one you agreed with, then yes, you would evaluate your journey by the amount of cash you have managed to amass. Or perhaps you would have a complex share portfolio system to help you work out your paper value (that is, the value of the shares you own). Then again, maybe your stocks are in private non-traded business which have no known value, but a value might be calculated periodically etc.?

Or, perhaps, this is all a big waste of time?

Certainly, it is a way to spend a lot of time, and to little purpose.

Equally, if you agree that you need to 'do it for the fun – the money is secondary' then perhaps you would choose 'fun' as the measure?

Fun may be a better measure than money, but it still has problems. A lot of business ventures are risky and scary whilst also being exhilarating and thrilling. Now, that may be a kind of fun, but it's an odd way of describing the trials and tribulations of business and overcoming them. Indeed when people say they love business, it is rarely the smoothness of the ride that, on reflection, most invigorated them. And fun isn't quite the right word for that.

So what then?

As you can imagine, we could continue this line of argument almost indefinitely and still be at no better definition of true business success. Every measure of externals has its problems.

Let me then propose an alternative way of dealing with this question.

An alternative approach

Instead of outcomes, let's take a look at your behaviour.

Now before I explain this, let me warn you – as if you needed warning – that to build a successful enterprise you have to get used to making and acting on tough decisions. You need to become as good at firing people as hiring people. You need to know when to cut your losses. You need to be able to disappoint people (although they might ultimately thank you) and move on.

You need – in the typical entrepreneurial vernacular – to be tough. But that doesn't mean you have to be hard or mean.

Here is the test, then.

If you can do everything you need to succeed as an entrepreneur, but in such a way as to retain your soul, then you are winning. Perhaps Saint Peter put it best when he wrote of "goodness… knowledge…self-control…perseverance…godliness… brotherly kindness…love".

These are the things that matter in a life, far and above the demands of business; and if you allow business to order them, rather than the other way round, you might as well try to blot out the sun in order to see better.

Measure your success by what good things you've stored up inside yourself and, come fortune or failure, the labour was never wasted.

* * *

So, the real test is this – firstly, can you do what needs to be done in order for your venture to have the opportunity of growing and succeeding? And, at the same time, can you retain self-control, kindness and everything else that matters?

The successful business will be led by someone who can manage that contradiction.

7.

Sharpen the saw

Sharpen the Saw is a famous axiom from Stephen Covey's *The Seven Habits of Highly Effective People*.

What does it mean?

You, the entrepreneur, started the business in your head a long time before anyone was hired. You took the bold step to inaugurate it; all the pluck and dare came from you. Another way to look at it is that you 'put up the risk'. That is, even if you didn't put an awful lot of money into the business, you took a brave decision and risked your time, energy and reputation to get the business going.

That means you don't have to accept the traditional pattern of 48 weeks' work and four weeks' holiday.

You need to lead the business. And you need to be sharp. Don't think you can be sharp all the time, so take time to take a break, do something else and sharpen the saw.

Do not keep normal office hours

It is important to establish, from early on, that you don't work normal 9-5 hours.

You can work 7 am to 6 pm if you wish. Or 10 am to 10 pm. You can vary it. But don't believe that you need to fit into a standard employee contract's hours.

As the leader of the business you'll attend late night business dinners and early morning networking breakfasts, so don't fall for the myth that you need to be at work every hour of the day.

I found this one of the hardest things to do. As the business grew, I felt that I needed to be in the office to make sure everyone else was working too. This wasn't surprising, really, as our monthly wage bill was hundreds of thousands of pounds – so I needed to make sure that the sales were coming in.

However, this approach didn't do me any good in the long run, and it didn't help my teams either.

It would have been better to have slimmed down the business costs to the point where it was always profitable by the end of the third week in every month.

If you set a goal to make a profit by the end of the third week, then you only need to turn up at the office at the end of week two and week three. You can let go of the need to know whether your staff are at their desks at nine in the morning or working past 5 pm. You can let go of all that, and allow yourself to keep irregular hours.

Of course, not keeping regular hours also means turning up on unexpected days. This is a great way to keep everyone on their toes – no one knows when you'll be in the office.

So get your business performing to the right measures and then you can stop worrying about clocking on and clocking off.

Go on holiday – and judge your business on your return

Taking a holiday and handing over the reigns to your team will teach both them and you a lot about where your business has got to.

If the business can run well without you, then you are ready to grow. If, on your return, you find a mess, then you know your team is not ready to take on more and you may want to review how your team is set up.

Of course, a mess may turn up whilst you are on holiday, and this may be no different from a typical week or month. However, the issue is whether your team was able to deal with the mess. And was the solution they came up with a better solution than you could have thought of? If so, you have a great team.

If not, then you need to solve the mess and find a better team.

Taking a holiday gives you a break and also teaches you, dispassionately, what your business is capable of. Just be willing to act on the basis of what you find when you return.

8.

Make your passion your business

Entrepreneurs' businesses usually grow out of their passions – and the successful ones nourish them. So, what are you passionate about? I'm passionate about publishing and media – that's why I write books, blogs and develop digital media businesses.

My previous business began as a publishing business but morphed into a property sourcing business and a property management business – neither of which I had a passion for. I ended up running the wrong kind of business, for me at least. It didn't work out because I wasn't passionate about the business anymore and didn't manage to find a capable and passionate manager to carry the business forward.

So, don't ignore this one. You can only put up with a business you are not passionate about for a very short time, particularly if you are a natural entrepreneur who always wants to move onto the next new project.

If you are not sure about a business or your passion for that business, check in with yourself and, if necessary, sell it.

Be passionate – even though others don't like it

All great entrepreneurs are passionate about what they do. And all entrepreneurs are called bullies at some point in their careers.

Do you have to be a bully to be an entrepreneur? Of course not.

Bullying is normally associated with abuse. The entrepreneurial workplace is a high performance, high-octane location. Anyone who joins a fast-growing business is assured a lot of excitement, opportunities to learn and a lot of change. Each team member will also know that their performance is key.

If this is not an environment that someone wishes to work in, then they are the wrong person for your team. This does not make you a bully and it does not make them wrong either. Simply make sure you are conveying this need in your recruitment, and have a clear and painless path to leave on for those who it does not suit.

Being passionate about what you do, and surrounding yourself with passionate people, is critical in an early stage start-up business. Don't let others undermine your passion for what you do.

The money has to be secondary

As an entrepreneur the end result can be a mountain of money so big you don't know what to do with it. But the early years will not bring this. The early years require self-sacrifice and paying others before you pay yourself.

Hence, you can't be an entrepreneur purely for the money. Somehow it has to be in your blood, or like actress Dame Judi Dench said about acting, "It was the only thing I could possibly do."

9.

Nothing but the truth – and quick

Tell it how it is – to your staff, your clients and your suppliers. Don't be offensive: be direct to the point of bluntness, but always gentle in your delivery. Most of all, tell them fast. The faster you tell them, the easier it is for them to meet and fulfil their objectives or overcome a problem.

Not telling people frankly and openly about a situation is a sure way to put a large hole into your enterprise and damage your reputation. Even bad news, shared openly and quickly, will put you in a position to recover the situation.

If you have managers or team members who struggle with this idea or are unable to articulate quickly and clearly then let them go; they are not right for your enterprise.

Generally I have found that bad news delivered in a soft voice is the best way. It forces you, the speaker, to breathe, and it forces the listeners to listen carefully and not jump to conclusions before you have finished. And yes, you can still be passionate and speak softly.

10.

Don't pin your hopes on a premature retirement

A favourite foolish goal of mine (foolish because, yes, I fell for it) is the "I want to retire by the time I am x." 40 was my goal, others set 30 or 50.

I've noticed that I've never seen a successful entrepreneur set this goal of premature retirement. Yes, successful entrepreneurs are either rich or old, and sometimes both – but never retired. Always, successful entrepreneurs want to be in the game and building businesses. If they ever leave the fray when of working age, they are not long in returning.

If you love what you do, why would you stop?

So, the reason young entrepreneurs set this goal is something to do with the fact that they are not enjoying what they are doing. In fact, the motivation for becoming an entrepreneur is often that they are not enjoying their job and becoming an entrepreneur would appear to be the solution. However, instead of embracing a lifelong commitment to growing profitable businesses, they set a foolish goal of retiring in five years' or 15 years' time.

None of this is realistic. You won't build an astonishingly successful business unless you love your work: mustering the sheer commitment just isn't possible without that passion. And if you love your work, you won't want to retire.

No, the early retirement goal is for those stuck in employment. If you are an entrepreneur, you don't need it. So ditch it.

Risk rises at the prospect

If quick retirement is set as the key goal then it will also lead to warped business decisions. Instead of balancing the growth of the business and its capital value with a desire to make profits (to be both reinvested and paid out to shareholders), it quickly leads to a bet-the-business mentality. All because of the desire to escape – sorry, retire!

I did this with my first business.

And guess what? Most team members, especially those with share options, will encourage you to go for the big gamble, too – just as our business advisors did as well. They risk very little if it fails, but stand to gain a lot if it succeeds. For you, the downside is much greater – and this is a key reason why share options don't work. They don't align the interests of the option holders with the shareholders. They create a 'heads I win, tails you lose' scenario (see Rule 96).

So don't be tempted by a big gamble and bet the business. And remember, being overly fixated on early retirement dangerously encourages you to take a bigger gamble.

11.

Never work to 'save jobs'

It sounds so good and wholesome to say you are working to save the jobs in your company, but it is the kiss of death for a business.

A business can only keep jobs if it is making profit. It is the absence of profit which forces jobs to be cut: therefore, the focus *must* be profit and not 'saving jobs'. Anyone (don't worry – I've done this often) who deludes themselves that they are working to save jobs is in fact, if they aren't lucky, sooner or later condemning the business to defeat.

If you really want to keep jobs, you'll make the focus on profit margin absolute and cut any roles that damage your profit margin. This may mean a smaller number of jobs, but they will be more secure and will allow you to reliably increase jobs in the future when the revenue growth of the business allows it.

Don't fall for the temptation to sound good and honourable – *be* good and honourable; do the right thing and take care of profit.

12.

Avoid the 'we've just got to survive the recession' fallacy

If you focus on merely surviving and arrange your business accordingly, the chances are – as with all aims, especially in recessions – that you'll fall slightly short of your goal sooner or later. And that little slip will spell disaster and, probably, bankruptcy.

You only have one choice and that is to cut back hard on business costs *and* grow the business. Yes, both things at once.

Of course, you might choose to grow profitability at the expense of revenue growth, but this is still growth. Your business is still growing in terms of its value even if the revenue is taking a sharp reduction. When you focus on avoiding the negative outcome (surviving the recession), you forget to focus on what is important and that is that you *have* to grow your business.

You need to get money back into marketing and generating new customers and making new sales.

You need to support your profit margins by supporting your brand and the value proposition of what you offer.

Avoid the 'market has disappeared' fallacy

Sometimes the market in which the business operates will simply disappear!

Okay, look, it isn't quite like that. What happens is that customer needs and wants shift and your business might be looking the wrong way. It is better to ask, "Where have my customers gone and how have the needs of those customers changed?"

In the 2008-09 recession, it was mid-price products and services that suffered the most. People who normally bought mid-priced cars, houses, holidays, clothes and food were forced to downsize and reduce their costs very fast, so they went for the low-cost options.

Equally, people who were not forced to downsize were sufficiently wealthy to live pretty much as they were doing before, and so continued to buy more expensive items. They didn't 'downgrade' to mid-price products. The mid-price customer just seemed to have vanished.

Or had it?

Recognising that it is a myth to say that 'markets disappear' gives you the opportunity to think about how the market has shifted and how to adjust your offering and products to fit the new environment. So, in the 2008-09 recession the use of discount coupons ballooned amongst savvy businesses as this allowed mid-market brands to offer low-end prices. This growth was in response to the market shift. The customers, in other words, hadn't disappeared, they had simply moved on, and it took the sellers a while to figure out how to reach them – with discounts!

13.

Proper profit is profit margin

Many entrepreneurs measure profit the wrong way. The key measure is profit *margin*, not pure profit.

Give a manager the responsibility for increasing profit from £100,000 to £200,000 and he or she may do it by selling four times more product at half the profit margin. This change in price strategy and profit margin will have a powerful impact on your brand. It may be a good temporary impact, but the overall effect will be long lasting and hard to reverse.

In particular, the thinner margin will make your business much more vulnerable to small swings in the cost of raw materials (or, say, an increase in government taxes on employment). Your business risks approaching a knife edge, whilst you reward your manager for doing 'a good job'.

Instead, make profit margin the key goal.

Avoid short-term profitability if at the expense of profit margin

As per the example above, it is easy to drive revenue (that's increase sales revenue) simply by slashing prices – at least for a short while. The real damage, however, doesn't become clear until later.

Many recession-hit enterprises slash prices to help keep revenue in tact. But customers grow accustomed to the discounts and time their purchases to coincide with the discount periods.

A discount, unless carefully managed, quickly becomes a permanent price reduction.

So what does this do to your business? Well, for example, a business on a 20% profit margin that cuts its prices by 10% and leaves its costs unchanged will see the margin fall to 11%.

Here's how it works:

I sell my product for £1, my costs are 80p and I have a 20% profit margin (20 / 100 = 20%).

Let's reduce my selling price by 10% to 90p. Now I have a 10p profit on a 90p sales price and that gives an 11% margin (10 / 90 = 11%).

So a modest discount – 10% – has almost halved the profit margin.

Clearly, if you carry on discounting you quickly won't have any profit at all.

It is better, instead, to accept lower revenue and maintain the profit margin, even though that means cutting your costs in line with falling revenue. In sharp downturns, this will require a sharp reduction in costs.

Yet, do you have the flexibility to reduce costs quickly without incurring significant 'change management' costs? That is, redundancy, cancelling office space contracts and so forth. If not, then your business has a problem and the solution is to start a move to contract and freelance staff now, before it is too late (see Rule 26).

A greater use of contractor and freelance skills – with the ability to turn on and turn off that resource – will allow you to keep profit margin in tact even when your revenues are falling. And, whilst this may shrink your business faster, it increases its ability to survive and subsequently grow again.

14.

The second goal of business is sustainability

Great – your business is taking off and revenues are flowing. You will soon be making a profit, too. That's excellent. Now, how sustainable is that growth?

- If your business is based on one or two customers then you are at risk should a single customer change their mind.

- If your revenues are dependent on a cyclical business cycle (property or recruitment, for instance) then your business will go up and down with the cycle.

- If the cost of adding new customers increases as you expand, then your profit margin will fall and you will need to stop growing.

- If the cost of maintaining your assets (machinery) or brands (advertising and marketing) is increasing then unless you have a comparable increase in sales or prices, your business is heading for the buffers.

- If your best staff keep leaving (top sales people for instance) and you are unable to replace them, then your business is going to start to lose money.

All of these examples are problems which confront businesses that lack sustainability.

As entrepreneurs we can get really excited about the revenue growth, we can see the cash in the bank increasing steadily too, but we may have built a business that is not sustainable. This kind of business is neither going to make long-term big profits nor achieve a great business sale value; if its profit making might only last three years and not ten or 20, it will only be worth a third or a sixth of an equally profitable business which *is* sustainable. (See Rule 17.)

Therefore, your goal as an entrepreneur must be to create and establish sustainable businesses – all business valuations or company dividends will depend on this.

What is sustainable?

Easy – a business which can expect to earn money and pay dividends for 20 years (rather than one or five) based on a powerful brand, franchise or piece of intellectual property (IP) is a sustainable business.

This level of sustainability will also determine how many sleepless nights you have and how hard you have to work. The more sustainable, the better you sleep. Unsustainable businesses require a huge effort just to keep the business going and above water. Sustainable businesses have a natural ability to grow, in effect, by themselves.

So, what is the best specific measure of sustainability? Well, a very good – but not perfect measure – is the revenue-per-employee (or equivalent) figure.

What is revenue per employee? It is your total gross revenue divided by your number of employees or equivalent employees.

So, if you are running your own business full time and have five freelancers, each of whom average one day per week of work for you, then you have two equivalent full-time employees.

Take your revenue – perhaps £50,000 – and divide by two, giving you £25,000 per employee.

Now, a strong, growing and mature company, such as Google, would expect revenue per employee of above £200,000.

Of course, a new business, with little revenue and just a founder working full time is going to have a low revenue per employee.

The point here is not the absolute figure but whether the revenue per employee is growing. If the revenue per employee is increasing, then you are building strength into your business (getting closer to a Google). If the figure is declining, then your business is weakening (getting closer to going bust).

The long-term future of your business will depend on your ability to increase the revenue per (or per equivalent) employee – albeit without using accounting tricks, such as moving some staff members 'off balance sheet' by outsourcing work.

15.

How to set a business-sale goal

Goals get in the way of selling businesses and banking profits. So, here are some things you must avoid and other things you must do.

Avoid the 'sell for £x' shareholder goal

A shareholder goal, 'sell for £x million within five years', is a typical if unwieldy goal that first-time entrepreneurs often set.

At the outset of an entrepreneurial career this goal might give your fellow partners a sense of excitement and enthusiasm; however, it is unlikely to engage any experienced investors. They will see this mainly as youthful exuberance. At this stage the goal is not harmful, other than the fact that it shows a lack of experience.

This lack of experience usually gets more dangerous when the young entrepreneur stands on stage in front of potential investors and says, "Give me £200k and I'll give you a £10m business." In truth, no experienced entrepreneur would ever make this kind of promise. And this goal can become highly destructive if it becomes enshrined in the shareholder agreement and without an end date.

Why? Well, if your business is successful and starts to grow, then the founders will quickly develop an expectation of achieving the goal. Yet, the business might not naturally grow quite to that level of profit or valuation in a short space of time.

Should the business do well – but not quite as expected – then shareholders are likely to become disappointed because their expectations are not being met, rather than be happy because they have backed a successful business.

This shareholder disappointment is likely to lead to some dangerous behaviour, such as replacing the founders, tearing up the profit margin rule and going for revenue growth, or seeking to sell at the top of the market (very risky) rather than banking a healthy profit early on.

Set an expiry date for business or shareholder goals

Shareholder goals are great when they galvanise the shareholders and managers (often the same people in a start-up company) to stretch to reach a specific goal, a sale, or a steady dividend income.

However, having established a strong goal in the first place, it is then very hard to change it to make the goal fit the reality of the business you have built and the desire to stay focused on profit margin not revenue (which is sometimes used to – badly – value businesses)!

So what is the solution? How do you use goals but not become fixated or constrained by them?

Firstly, give your goal an annual review in which the shareholders can vote to change it. Secondly, in case you can't reach an agreement with the shareholders as to a target right now, set a date further ahead – say in three years' time – when the goal will expire.

When you reach three years hence, the shareholders can either agree a new goal or that there is no goal. With this approach, shareholders will come to an agreement that is much more likely to reflect the realities of the position of the business within the overall business cycle. And, of course, it helps greatly to keep expectations in place.

Of course, if you don't have other shareholders, then you don't need to manage at this level of detail. However, it is still important to engage the interest of your senior managers and show a path to an exciting business-growth target. Therefore, even if this business remains entirely in your control, you should still set and communicate this goal – and that it has an expiry date.

Sell your business when you are winning awards

The best time to sell a business is at the top of the business cycle but even more so when everyone is congratulating you on building a brilliant business.

The point is not so much the obvious one (your business now looks, justly, attractive) but that if everyone else has noticed what a great business you have, you will soon be facing a snowstorm of competitors and pressure on your profit margins.

Your business may be able to defend itself and still grow, but it will become harder work.

This is the point when most entrepreneurs should exit. It is always better to leave the party at the height of the festivities than to be one of the last to leave.

16.

Run the business for dividends (shareholder profit)

If you start a business, then it is your baby. If it grows up, you get to become the father or mother figure to the staff and suppliers and you feel important. It is easy at this stage to forget that you have two roles – running the business and maximising shareholder returns (or shareholder profit). So, let's take a look at shareholder returns.

People get confused about shareholder returns. Terribly confused – I know I had a horrible time with them.

There is only one real measure of shareholder return, and that is how much money the business will pay out in dividends and for how long. The shareholders can decide to take none of the profit right now (which would come in the form of a dividend) and instead reinvest everything in the hope of a sale of the business for big money later on. Alternatively, shareholders can decide to run the business for short-term profit ("Pay out as much money as you can while the going is good, it won't last!") and accept the business will ultimately sell for very little. Or, finally, they can take out a proportion of the profits as dividends and leave a proportion for reinvestment.

You can see which the most sensible path is – and yes, it is the middle path of paying out some profit and keeping some profit to reinvest.

The decision about the balance – 80/20, 20/80, or anything in between – will come down to a decision about the potential of any reinvestment.

Essentially, if a £1 reinvested now can pay a shareholder 10p per year for 20 years (as an increased profit and the resulting shareholder dividend) then this is a good reinvestment for the shareholder.

In all cases such as this – reinvest £1 and get £2 in return, the decision is easy – reinvest.

Equally, if a business asks its shareholders to reinvest £1 and get 10p per year for 10 years – a total of £1 – then the shareholders should ask for the money to be paid out in the form of dividends instead. There is no point in waiting 10 years to get paid the £1 you could be paid right now.

Therefore, the decision of how to balance the reinvestment versus dividend payout will ultimately depend on the confidence that the reinvestment will increase the shareholder dividend and for how long that increase will last.

Hence, the rule here is that, at all times, the business is run for shareholder profit, despite the fact that shareholders may choose to delay some profit in order to reap larger rewards in the future.

Keep salary and dividend conversations apart

It is easy to confuse salary and dividend, especially when the salary earners also hold shares.

In my previous business this got horribly confused because all the shareholders were also full-time directors who were also paid salaries. The pay between the directors varied greatly – the sales director, for example, was paid four times what the IT director was – and the ownership of dividend-bearing shares was also quite different from the shareholdings.

The sales director was able to preserve a self-employed basis and earn part of his income via a Cypriot company. The result was that the sales director wanted to earn more money as salary, whilst the

IT director wanted to get paid dividends as he had already reached the UK upper tax threshold limit.

What a mess!

I found myself attempting to navigate a whole series of personal incentives – all made more complex and opaque by curious personal tax structures – my own included – which resulted in the business not paying out dividends.

One solution is to ensure that there is only one shareholder, or if you take on other shareholders, that you take on those shareholders for their cash injection (and occasional advice) only. You do not, therefore, have a complex mix of shareholders who are also paid for full-time roles (part-time non-exec directorships are okay if modestly paid).

Therefore, you can stay focused on what is best for SHAREHOLDERS – and put their interests first.

Lastly, if shareholders are not receiving a dividend of any kind and the business is growing, then the shareholders would be advised to sell. It would be wise to include such an option in any shareholder agreement whereby the shareholders can sell their stakes to anyone of their choice without offering tag-along rights (that is, ensuring that they can sell their own shares without regard to other shareholders – Rule 91) if they don't receive dividends of at least 5% of turnover. This option will greatly help motivate a management to pay dividends and therefore ensure that shareholders are also rewarded as well as the management team (who will typically hold fewer shares but earn large salaries).

17.

Use the dividend cash flow to value your business

Valuing a business is, contrary to most opinions, very easy.

The value of your business is the amount of money that your business can pay out as a shareholder dividend for as long as the business can pay it out. So, if your business pays out a total of £500 in shareholder dividends every year for ten years and then collapses, the business is worth £5000 – okay, with some minor adjustments for inflation.

There you go, we've just shown that great and complex ideas can be expressed simply.

Hopefully we've also highlighted, again, how important steady dividends are? Make that 20 years of dividend instead of ten and suddenly the business is worth twice as much for the same annual dividend.

Remember, dividends are paid out of a business's profit – where some of the profit is kept back to be reinvested in the business (more on that later).

18.

Focus on cash-flow forecasts

What is hard in business forecasting is figuring out what your future cash flow will be. It is much easier to forecast sales volumes, so this is how we should start to work out our cash flow.

Using industry-standard profit margins as your base, you can begin to forecast cash flow. For example:

> If you are forecasting a sales volume of £100,000, and the industry-standard profit margin is 10%, then your forecast costs will be £90,000.

> Now work out if your costs fall before, after or at the point of banking your sales revenue; and what they are; and then you will have a decent cash-flow forecast.

Of course, you will be told (or it will be tempting to tell yourself) that if you had more revenue you could make more profit – but don't fall for this beguiling line. A sudden rush of sales volume can easily take place if we let go of the profit margin, as we saw earlier.

Therefore, stick to the principle that profit margin comes first, and with the expectation that your CEO (or yourself) will achieve at least the industry-standard profit margin *then* you can ask what sales you can achieve.

With the knowledge of sales volume and profit margin, you can now calculate your dividend, and from this your business value (see Rule 17).

19.

Check your bank balance daily

Your cash position is so important that you should look at your bank account daily – or, if you have more than one account, ask your finance team to give you a simple figure. How much cash is in the account(s)?

Now, to make this a useful figure, ask your accounts to give you the same figure from one year ago and how much it has gone up (or down).

This very simple rule will give you plenty of insight into the performance of your business.

20.

Don't do guilt

Yes, lots of people will try to make you feel guilty about profit and, yes, this is why we often pretend that the business isn't there to make a profit.

Look, we know this is rubbish – so let's just not accept the guilt. We know that everything in the business ultimately depends on profit (or, as we saw earlier, profit margin). If team members want exciting jobs and career advancement, they will only come about if we make profit and hold strong profit margins. The more we make and the bigger the margin, the more exciting it will be.

And, as for your rewards as the founder, remember (as earlier) that all the risk in starting the business was, by and large, yours. So what you do with the money is your choice – spend it, save it or give it away if you like – but don't feel guilty about it.

Earn your profit, take your profit, declare your profit and then, if you choose, put it to good work building new businesses or donate it to someone who can make a bigger difference with it than you can.

But please, we don't have time for guilt.

21.

Beg, borrow and barter

If you follow the old advice to never borrow, then you will have limited or perhaps no cash available.

So, begin your enterprise by begging, borrowing or bartering. That is, if you can't persuade someone to give you what you need for free, then see if they will loan it to you – perhaps for some share of upside – or offer to provide a useful service to them in return.

Perhaps you can offer some free promotion in return for office space, advice or help with the accounts? More ambitiously, if you cannot pay for your accounts, why don't you offer to introduce four new clients to your accountant for free instead?

Of course, it's important that you can deliver at least one paying customer up-front, as this will immediately establish your credibility. And given that your accountant, like all businesses, will spend between 10 and 50% of their income on marketing to reach new and existing customers, your offer may be very welcome. If you can deliver four new clients to them per year, then the chances are that the value of the saving on marketing and finding those new clients each year will be equivalent to the cost of providing you with the same service for the whole year.

22.

Use win/win negotiation

Young entrepreneurs sometimes interpret the advice to beg, borrow or barter as a recommendation to try to get everything for free and offer nothing in return. This is a very bad approach.

Instead, in this as in all your business negotiations, you must seek to understand what the other person wants. It should be, for want of a less cheesy name, win/win negotiation.

And it should be applied not only in the begging-borrowing-bartering phase of start-up, but always – to relations with your staff, discussions with your suppliers, and so on (everyone, in short). This doesn't mean surrendering your own objectives, but rather understanding the simple function of human nature, often overlooked: that it is much easier to get your way if you are helping others get their way at the same time.

Reject all long-term agreements that aren't win/win

The one thing I have learned is that any negotiation in which I win, but the other side loses, always ends in disaster. Yes, you can force people into a corner where they have to accept your deal, but you'll probably make an enemy of them in the process – and that will store up problems for the future.

Of course, a win/win negotiation must also mean that you don't bend too far and end up with a bad deal yourself. Which leaves us with one last option…to walk away.

The walk-away negotiation rule

The option to walk away is a great way to save face and end a negotiation that is not proceeding as you might hope. Both parties can leave with their respect in tact, if you walk away early enough, and this always leaves room to renegotiate again in the future. It also means that you don't waste your or anyone else's time.

Showing that you are willing to walk away can also be a great way of allowing the other side to make one last effort to reach an agreement that works for both of you. However, if the other party does come back, remember not to negotiate them down too hard, as you must leave sufficient profit or other incentive for them to want to deliver a quality piece of work.

Ultimately, a poor or average piece of work is not worth anything anyway and will damage your business either immediately or in the long run. Therefore, don't allow agreements where the provider doesn't care about the quality of the outcome. Typically this means that it is better to be a medium-sized client of a small firm than a tiny client of a very large firm.

Don't knock down the price

The other approach inexperienced negotiators follow is to attack the price. This is generally an awful idea as it will quickly reduce any negotiation to a "you're not worth that", "yes I am", "no you are not" type negotiation.

In my experience, this is not negotiation, but simply an attempt at mutual suicide.

It might work if you are attempting to buy a discounted house and have 100 properties to choose from – when you are rejected, you simply move to the next one – but it never works with business partners, freelancers or service providers, because the value of the work depends on motivation and the quality of the relationship.

So, if someone says that they are worth £15 per hour or £250 per hour, then ask them to demonstrate it by giving them a project to quote on. That is, write down what you want to achieve, and then ask them how they would achieve it and what it would cost. Then you'll have a clear idea of whether it is better to hire the freelancer at £250 per hour for a single hour (total cost £250) or the junior at £15 per hour for a whole week (total cost £525).

If you like the quote, and want to get more value, then seek to add additional deliverables but try to meet their demand on the price. So, if you are quoted £500 for a project, see if you can add some other valuable services into the overall quote. This method of adding up, rather than knocking down, will show that you respect the person you are working or contracting with. It shows that you don't dispute that they are worth what they say, and so you negotiate about what they will do, rather than what or who they are.

23.

Deliver your promises up-front

If you promise to deliver a service in return for help – or bartering – then you must be prepared to deliver up-front. Why? Well, you are either the unproven entrepreneur or starting out with an unproven idea. And you will be asking to hire services from established businesses.

Therefore, as we saw already, it is ill advised to say, "If you prepare my accounts for one year, and I'm happy with the service, then I'll get you four new clients" – you will be laughed at.

Instead, as said before, aim to deliver a new customer straight away and then promise to bring three more if you reach an agreement. This approach will demonstrate that you are not only a capable negotiator but also likely to be a highly valuable client and source of future business.

Delivering on your promises – quickly and without fuss – is a great way to build credibility. An accountant is not only going to be impressed by the new client but he or she will also be thinking that you might grow a big and successful business.

And, of course, all accountants or lawyers like to see their clients grow – it is good for their business too.

Hence, establishing that you can deliver what you say you can deliver will change the way that people treat you immediately. Life will get a lot easier.

And, you know what, even if you don't deliver everything you set out to deliver right away you will at least have demonstrated that you are willing to put some hard work in and keep going until you get the results you promised. This willingness buys a lot of credibility and it is how you win people over, and begin to establish yourself and your new business.

24.

Keep collaborating

Many entrepreneurs start life with no cash, a huge burning desire and a willingness to trade, barter and collaborate with other companies. As the business grows and more competitors start to attack their markets, there is a natural tendency to stop collaborating. This is a mistake.

Instead, simply look to collaborate with larger companies that have established themselves or people that convince you that they are worth believing in.

We often make the mistake of believing we have to defend our business once it has grown a bit.

I have come to the view that when everyone wants to copy your ideas, the only solution is not to hide your ideas away, but simply to raise the bar on innovation and collaboration within your market. Or sell.

If you can innovate faster and more effectively – in both your products and services as well as in your collaborative relationships – then your competitors won't be able to keep up with you. So they'll give up and go away, eventually.

So keep collaborating, even when you begin to enjoy some success.

25.

Run a 'to-stop' list

You keep a 'Things to Do' list, don't you?

Well, do you also keep a 'Things to Stop' list, too? You should – and so should your staff. And what goes onto it should receive just as regular thought as the to-do list.

A stop-doing list is a list of things that you've been doing that are having no material impact on the success of the business. Typically these are activities that either were a good idea but never worked out or are old processes or ways of doing things which have now been replaced by changes in the way the business works or by new software or different seating arrangements.

A good example is this: one member of my team was responsible for keeping the customer records correct and up to date. Sounds great? Well, this became a matter of the following:

- filing every client email in a separate folder on Microsoft Outlook

- printing out each email and filing that in a folder

- copying each email to a shared drive and replicating the filing in a digital format.

In addition, the email systems and shared drives were backed up every evening – so we effectively had five copies of every client email.

Yes, it is good to have backups, but five copies in three formats? The cost of this system was enormous in terms of manpower and, as it turned out, a near complete waste of time and resources.

When the person left, no one even used the digital filing – only a bit of rummaging around a filing cabinet.

Parkinson's Law

Parkinson's Law states that work expands to fit available time.

When the business profit margin is reduced, the argument against cuts to a person's budget is, invariably, that they have too much work already. The solution is to remember Parkinson's Law and recall that when you make a cut and the time shrinks, so, amazingly, can the work.

Equally, if you cut back on staff levels, then you should expect to see an increase or at least a stable 'revenue per employee' measure. This will mean that your business is remaining as strong or getting stronger as a result of the cuts, even though the business may now be smaller.

A strong business can learn to grow quickly when circumstances allow.

26.

Freelance is best

The majority of a modern business's day-to-day costs will be staff costs.

Therefore, if you are to build a business with a strong and stable profit margin – and that is the purpose, after all, of all good business practice – then who you hire / contract and how you hire them (and whether you keep them), and how you apply their skills and talent, will be the most important decisions you and your managers will ever make. They are also decisions that you need to reconsider and evaluate on a day-to-day basis.

However, before we get into the detail of how to manage staff for business success, let me explain why I believe that the fast growth businesses of the future will rely on freelance and contract staff either entirely or at least to a significant degree.

Freelancers and contract workers (even if they sit in your office all day long like full-time staff) generally deliver better value and create less friction than traditionally employed staff.

I learned this the hard way. At the point when my first business was at greatest stress, the freelancers and contractors behaved in a mature and grown-up fashion, with a shared desire to do whatever was necessary to make the business work. The employees – or at least a small number of employees – took a different approach. And, despite a number responding as positively as the freelancers, that small querulous minority made it impossible to continue with the business.

In essence, when we had to reduce staff and move our teams from fixed salaries and payments to a structure more closely related to the actual revenues being achieved (as opposed to the revenue forecast), the freelancers understood and were prepared to take on the challenge. A handful of employees refused. The employees were within their legal rights, and therefore there was no basis for complaint. However, the effect was to make the business untenable for everyone – the contractors, the employees who were willing to be flexible as well as those who were not, and the freelancers too. It was game over.

Now, it would be preposterous to tar all salaried employees of all companies with the same brush. The point is not that all employees will create these difficulties (most won't); it's that only a handful need to, at a critical time, in order to cause you and your business a monumental and possibly fatal problem.

The difference can be summed up by saying that freelancers and contractors had a grown-up relationship with the issues and the business – and we dealt with the difficulties like two adults – whereas, a minority of employees took a parent-and-teenager approach, where they expected the business to bail them out and keep them afloat no matter what they did.

Therefore, assuming that all businesses will face a difficult period sooner or later, if you do not have all or a large majority of your team on a freelance / contract structure, then you will find yourself with a team who *could* adopt a troublesome teenager-like attitude and demand their rights rather than a team who wants to work alongside you to find a way through any difficult patch.

Now, having stated my position and my earnest recommendation that you build a business based largely on freelance teams, you may already have large employed teams that you can't afford or legally are not allowed to restructure. Therefore, we need to deal with the mistakes that are made in regards to traditional employment too. However, these points are also relevant to hiring and working with freelance and contractual staff, only the issues are less likely to arise and are usually simpler to deal with (after all, that's precisely the point of why freelance and contractual staff are better).

27.

Hire freelancers correctly

If you find the notion of firing staff for underperformance unpalatable, then your alternative, again, is to solely hire freelance or contract staff. At the end of the contract the contractor leaves without dispute or disagreement.

If both parties wish to continue, then they can either write a new contract or take a break for a period of time and then subsequently write a new contract when ready.

Remember, the advantage of your freelancer taking a break and working elsewhere, if they are local, is that they will widen and deepen their experience at another firm. This means that if you re-hire in six months or six years, they will have gained new skills and knowledge that can help your business – and you didn't have to fund the training course.

Freelancers working in your office

Many entrepreneurs are under the false impression that freelance and contract staff cannot work in their office. This is false. A contracted member of your team can work in your office if you contractually require it.

Typically, you will allow freelance staff to work from home if they are working on an independent project or just part time. When the project becomes time-sensitive or a complex team project, or even if there are problems with the work (e.g. it is more complex than you thought), then you will want them in your office.

However, you do need to be aware that contractual staff working five days a week in your office may be treated – for legal reasons – as full-time employees, owing to the dreaded IR35 legislation. There are some important things you can do to prevent this risk, such as ensuring that your contracts are for fixed periods and are not indefinite. You might also want to look into the possibility of hiring your contractors via an off-shore umbrella company. The important thing here is to get some sound advice based on current accepted practice as this is an area under constant change and development.

28.

Constantly question whether you have the right people in the right roles

The entrepreneur's key objective must be to know and understand all the potential resources that are available to them and their firm both right now and in the immediate future.

Why?

As your business grows, you will be able to do less and less of the day-to-day activity. You will, therefore, become increasingly dependent on growing a team of reliable people around you.

The ability to grow a team, focus a team, prune a team and re-grow a team is an extremely difficult set of skills to master. Yet it is these skills that you must learn – they will mean the difference between remaining a small businessperson and becoming a successful entrepreneur with a range of businesses.

Of course, each entrepreneur will develop his or her own style. That's okay. The key factor in all successful approaches, however, is that the entrepreneur will *constantly focus and constantly question whether they have the right people on board and in the right roles.*

There is no magic formula for this other than careful planning and using all the recruitment tools you can; as well as some good old hard work and trial and error. Research by Michigan State University tells us that only 14% of our hiring decisions (by interview alone, at any rate) work out for the long term. This is why it is critical to your enterprise to maintain a flexible employment structure, as this allows you to deal with your errors quickly (yes, you will make them) and without a cost that will destroy your business.

If you are in a new and evolving industry, as many entrepreneurial businesses are, then this flexibility – along with a willingness to use it – will make the difference between becoming a successful company and falling by the wayside.

It doesn't much matter here whether you are working with contractors/freelancers or full-time staff – in both cases you will constantly need to re-evaluate whether you have the right person in the right role. However, my experience to-date has been that freelancers will tell me that they are in the wrong role before I realise it, but employees will not.

The consequences of this are that the freelancers usually work out the solution themselves – move to another role or find another contract. Employees have a greater tendency to bury their heads in the sand. Therefore, if you are managing a full-time employee team you may have to spend much more of your time questioning whether you have employed the right people than you would with your freelance staff.

29.

Hire better than you need

So what is the staffing solution for a young growing business?

Well, to distil it into a single principle it has to be: Hire people who are better than you or your manager.

Why? Simple – because, as the role grows, they will get better and better, whereas you (or your manager) cannot hope to constantly stay ahead of all your staff or team (and nor would you want to).

And the test of whether someone is better than you is this: *When discussing their area of work, do you find that they train you or explain how things work? Or are you always training them?* If they are constantly adding to your knowledge, then they are better than you. If the reverse, they are weaker than you.

So, how do you hire people who are better than you when you can only afford junior staff?

Easy – you hire them for one day per week, on a senior rate, until you can afford to buy more time. This way you bring high levels of experience and knowledge into your business from day one, with immense capacity to grow.

Can this work for all kinds of businesses and roles? Well, pretty much yes. If you have too much admin or need the occasional phone call answered, there are plenty of virtual PA services out there. And generally, when you hire freelance PA services, you are still hiring someone with considerable experience who, given the freelance nature of the work, is often over-qualified for the general admin that needs to be done. But, because you are a client – and the experienced PA doesn't see this as a career issue – the work gets done with little or no fuss and great speed.

Okay, someone has to physically empty the bins – and you will pick up these jobs in the early days. But if you really don't want to clean the office toilet, just take a serviced office where these things will be done for you (and be prepared to pay the extra cost).

Can you really hire for the upper echelons of the business on this basis as well? (Say, a top quality manager on one day a week?) Well, think beyond the average job for the moment and consider the role of non-executive directors in large global companies. These directors work for a variety of different businesses and are not full time in any one. Does their part-time involvement make them a weaker part of those teams? Absolutely not!

And if you could get just one day per month from a senior non-exec director to guide your business would you really turn him or her down?

Many growth businesses are based in incubators attached to universities or research institutes. These places, even if you are not actually based there, will be full of capable and experienced managers who are used to working with a large number of start-up businesses – on a casual, one-day-a-week basis or similar.

To think that you can't hire top quality people on a one-day per week basis is simply an example of small thinking. The world of hiring skills and talents into your business really has changed and it is critical that you take advantage of these changes if you want to succeed. Hiring slightly over-qualified staff builds a capacity for growth into the very DNA of your business.

Expect excellence every day

A commitment to excellence in business means getting excellent performance out of your team and that means the right person, in the right job, at the right time.

The time can change, the job can change, and even if the job and timing remain the same, then the person might change (i.e. they lose the motivation or excitement that used to make them a great performer, which is particularly the case in high pressure or sales roles).

Hence, there is a myth that a good employee is always a good employee, and this mistake often goes to the heart of why entrepreneurs and business people keep staff on long after they have ceased to make a positive contribution to the business.

The reality is that new personal objectives and motivation come into play. The job will change and your business, as it grows, will shift from a small start-up – where the individual is involved in everything – to a major organisation, where their role is shrunk and compartmentalised.

In this case, if your team member is no longer as motivated as before, then the best thing for your staff member is to go and find another start-up (perhaps your next venture) – it would be good for them and good for you.

Equally, a staff member's personal work motivation can change. This is particularly true in sales teams.

Just make sure that you, as the manager, don't hold on to them for too long based on what they used to do or in the hope that they might find their spark again. If you can, quickly move them into a new role to fire up their motivation again. But equally, avoiding the tough decisions doesn't do you or them any favours in the long run and just builds up resentment. If they have lost their hunger or bite, then you can even invite them to take three or six months off, and yes, that might mean turning down new business due to a lack of staff.

Remember, it is more important to keep the excellence in your teams at a peak than it is to attempt to solely maximise sales. This is not because sales and revenue aren't important – they are, very – it is just that you can't expect to grow revenues unless you are willing to instil excellence into what you and your team do.

Sometimes, you will need to take a modest step backwards before you can move forwards strongly again.

Don't tolerate bad (or average) performance

It might surprise you to learn – and it really surprised me, too – that the real reason that great people leave a business is because average or bad performance is tolerated.

Don't believe me? Well, read this:

> "… collapse is a consequence of the firm's own success. Once it grows big enough, it becomes a haven for free-riders who capitalise on the efforts of others. So the firm becomes gradually riddled with slackers, until suddenly the other workers decide they have had enough and jump ship."

Philip Ball's discussion of *Axtell's model of why businesses fail*, in
Critical Mass

Shocking, isn't it?

This means that, as the manager, spending your time and energy attempting to turn around the performance of your weaker team members is a mistake. Instead, it is important to focus on the best people, helping them to excel, and replacing the weaker staff.

If you don't want the best to leave in exasperation, then you cannot afford to tolerate bad or average performance.

You may have noticed that I have only allowed for three types of performance: Excellent, Average or Poor. Be careful that your managers don't start talking about 'good' performance; make sure, instead, that this is interpreted as Average performance unless there is a strong reason to upgrade it. See Rule 41 for more on this.

30.

Grow only as fast as your resources allow

The other side of delegating to people who are better than you is that it often takes time to find that kind of quality recruit in the first place. A number of people you start work with won't deliver as you might have expected. This gets much worse if you are forced to grow at a fast pace.

If you find you have a shortage of the right level of skill (and you want excellence, right?) then you need to cut back on your business commitments. Yes, it is tough, but it is better to turn business away if you are unable to maintain your high standards than to persist if you know it requires the recruitment of weaker staff or team members.

Tough, I know, but if you can do it, and build this principle into the heart of your business, then you will ultimately build a very strong enterprise.

Recruit before growth

It is a mistake to recruit to meet growth. Instead, you should recruit because you have found the right person and then deliver the growth to take up the cost.

In truth, if you assemble a very powerful team you are likely to find that the high quality work will find you. If you do the opposite and only recruit when you have an urgent need, you will recruit in a hurry when you don't have the fullness of time to hire and are likely to make more mistakes than usual when hiring.

Yes, this feels counter-intuitive, and it is – but gathering around you a team of experts, even if you don't have a role for them immediately, is by far and away the most sustainable choice.

Okay, what about cash flow you might say? Or what about holding onto these people when they have nothing to do all day?

If you are asking yourself these questions then you are still thinking 'employees'.

The solution to the cash-flow argument is to hire from a broad freelance and contract base. Do this and yes, you can recruit before you grow. Fail to do this and yes, you will be bust before you make a sale.

The problem of panicking managers

Many jobs get placed and people get hired in a hurry because there is 'too much work'. A manager will often ask desperately for more resources, and no, they will tell you, they can't improve the process unless they can free up some time.

In a fast-growth business, managers who give you the "can't improve before I have more resources" argument are going to get you into trouble.

Now, in some cases, your manager may have a point. The trouble is that it is extremely hard to judge. So, do you start looking for a new manager or do you provide the extra resources (before you see any increase in improvement)?

In many cases, you may not have a choice. And your response may be: There are no extra resources; let's find a different way of doing what we need to do with what we have.

However, as per the point in Rule 29, don't spend your precious business time on weaker team members who aren't delivering. Instead, look around your business and find the managers who are coping on the resources that you are able to provide.

In this case, you have the option of helping the manager who is panicking by moving some of his or her work to another member of the team. I have found that this is often the best way to find out if the panic is solvable or not. Clearly, if a manager allows or encourages you to take their work away and give it to another manager who is able to cope, then it quickly becomes clear which manager is delivering excellence. And you know what you might need to do.

If that same manager comes to you yet again and says. "I need more staff or resources," the answer may well be, "Yes, and I need a new manager."

31.

Hire hunger (humble and hardworking), not the best (proud and expensive)

The related mistake is to believe that you must hire 'the best' staff. Well, who are the best staff?

In the years running up to 2007 many businesses falsely believed they were in a 'war for talent'. As if talent were like gold or oil and could be possessed.

The best staff or contractors are often those people hungry to progress, and therefore they may be starting on lower salaries because their lack of experience or qualifications does not enable them to get paid the big bucks. Some high paid staff with a good track record may be burned out or have lost their hunger. This can be apparent at the point of recruitment or it can take place after one, two or five years in the job.

Therefore, don't assume the recruitment interview will reveal which are 'the best staff'. You can only find this out by seeing what they produce, which is another excellent reason for hiring on a freelance or contractor basis.

If you worry – will the best agree to a contractual basis? – remind yourself that you do not want the 'best'. You are looking for those that are hungry for success and hardworking. Give them an opportunity which no one else will offer, and will they have an issue about a freelancer or contractor legal basis? Not at all.

32.

Pay the right price for the person

The old saying 'if you want monkeys, pay peanuts' has its place, but often it is used by employees or recruitment consultants to justify higher than normal salaries or fees. Most entrepreneurs forget that the price of peanuts rises and falls as well. This means that in boom times you will pay more and during a recession you will pay less.

Therefore, what you pay is principally about what is happening in your local market. Hence, if you don't like the price or the quality on offer, you have a few choices.

You can:

- wait until the supply is better

- look outside your local market or move to a lower-cost location

- find more supply – by increasing your pool of freelance people.

Why young businesses struggle to recruit from within – and how to solve it

Young businesses that grow rapidly face two recruitment issues:

1. a very small staff pool from which to promote

2. a rapidly developing business need.

So, to grow the staff pool without growing overheads means only one thing – building a much larger pool of freelance and contract staff.

Equally, when creating a new role, it is better to put a contractor into that role for a fixed term of six or 12 months. If the role becomes established as a value-generating (i.e. profitable) role, then the role can become permanent.

Separately, then, you can ask yourself who is the right person to fill that role, now that it has become permanent. Don't think that because the role is profitable and valid the person who set up the role is the right person to fill the ongoing position; often they are not. If you have a star performer who can set up new roles, it is better to move that person onto a new role, perhaps setting up a new division. If you left them where they are, what reward for performance would that be?

Use senior interim managers in entrepreneurial businesses

If your business is entrepreneurial and creating new ways of doing business or new services, then it is unlikely that someone else is already doing something similar. So hired senior managers who come from outside your business are unlikely to be able to help you resolve the problem of a weak team without huge upheaval and the risk of making matters worse.

So what you are looking for is a *very* experienced manager who can manage *unknown* change. Again, interim senior freelance management talent may have a better chance at solving these issues for growth businesses – not least because you have the opportunity of hiring someone who is more senior than the job. Whilst senior interim managers are expected to be more senior than the role, this is not typical with career/fully employed managers.

In addition, an interim should be more or less immediately available and therefore able to deal with the underlying issues quickly, whereas to recruit a senior manager from an existing position is a six to 12 month task. And you can't afford to wait that long.

33.

Never over-promote

Too many staff at small businesses get over-promoted because of the difficulty of hiring career managers into a growing business. I've highlighted the difficulty of recruiting in previous rules, but the solution, although tempting, is not to over-promote your existing team.

Promotion often serves to inflate the ego but fails to be matched with an increase in performance. Don't over-promote – especially early on. As we'll see, there are better options.

Acting-up roles and splitting roles

You can, for instance, offer acting promotional roles, which should be on a contract basis with no certainty of renewal.

Acting-up allows someone to assume a more senior role without being confirmed in that role. It allows you to set some very clear objectives for that more senior role to be confirmed and to establish that, if those objectives are not met, the seniority will be taken away. In this case, if the team member does not deliver the key objectives, they can revert to their previous role.

Now, do not think that failing to confirm someone in a new role is going to be easy. It is not, and the team member may leave if not confirmed – but at least they leave, rather than you having to create a false redundancy (with all the rights of their previous role carried forward at the new higher rate of pay) to solve the error.

Another way is to split the senior role and share the additional responsibility between two people. You can always select the stronger performer as the ultimately successful candidate.

Take responsibility before it's too late

It is much harder taking away responsibility than it is to give it. And the task only gets harder with time. Therefore, you must act early and quickly if the objectives are not met.

Use a career-tracking recruitment agency for senior staff

If you're going to hire senior staff from outside your organisation then you need to find a specialist agency. Don't adopt the normal approach of using a high street recruitment firm or placing an advert in the paper; it almost certainly won't work.

You need to find an agency that has been tracking the careers of a number of people for a large number of years, because they should be able to vouch for anyone they put forward.

The person you take on must have excellent references. This doesn't mean that they will have an impeccable record – many great senior staff became great by making some big mistakes, so don't ignore these men and women.

34.

Meet the spouse for senior roles

A senior manager will not be effective if his or her partner is not behind the appointment.

A senior manager will work long hours and travel away from home. It may also be necessary for them to relocate. All three factors will put significant pressure on their partner and family, so the family need to be supportive of the new role, and thus you must meet the family before you appoint.

This is particularly true if the relocation is to a foreign country (even more so if non-English speaking), where the partner left at home is at risk of becoming isolated and lonely.

35.

Use references early in recruitment

Many people lie on their CVs – to some extent.

Perhaps they claim a piece of work was delivered by them, whereas it was actually delivered by a team of which they were a member. This distinction can make a huge difference to their ability to repeat the success for your company. Therefore, take up references and take time to verify what are, for you, the key achievements and experiences they boast of.

When entrepreneurs (and businesses in general) do take up references, this is usually after a second-round interview. At this point the reference check is typically to ensure that there is no obvious reason *not* to hire this person. This is not as effective a use of the references as possible; in effect the decision has already been made, and all that insight goes wasted. Instead, take up references before the first interview (if less than six candidates) or after the first interview (if more candidates).

Be aware that you will need to get permission from the candidates for this, as they will probably not expect their current employer to be alerted to their job hunt at a point in the process where their appointment elsewhere is so tentative. Again, this demonstrates why freelancers are easier to deal with, as their current customers won't mind taking your phone call and they won't mind you making it.

The purpose of taking up the references earlier than usual is to:

- verify the level of duties performed

- verify the dates and the salary

- verify if there was any question of honesty and integrity

- the 'can they do your job' killer question.

Most people taking up references will ask the referee the first three questions, but probably one more question: "Would you employ this person again?"

However, this last question fails to address the really important question: "Would you hire this person again *in a more senior role than the one they were in*?"

Why do you want to ask this question? Simple – staff move jobs invariably for one of the following reasons:

- to gain more money than they are currently offered

- to win a promotion denied to them at their current job

- got fired/were being pushed out/were worried about job

- want to work for a different type of company and/or in a different industry or due to family relocation.

If they are moving jobs due to relocation, then they won't be expecting an increase in pay and may actually be willing to take a cut in pay, but you would still want to make sure that the previous employer would be willing to hire them again.

The other reason for someone switching jobs is because they want to 'get on' and earn more money and achieve greater promotion. Why weren't they able to achieve this at their previous employer or client?

Now, there may be a good reason for this – but you want to know it, and you also want to know what the previous employer or client thought. Without this kind of information it is likely that you will continue to make recruitment errors 86% of the time – as per the average highlighted by Michigan University in recruitment by interview alone.

36.

Avoid job titles

When a business is small and not paying the highest wages it is tempting to offer big job titles instead.

Of course, all team members want to have big job titles as it makes them feel good, but be careful – once given it is very hard to take one away. If you have a director of a £50k-turnover business, you will have to fight to be able to hire a senior manager (another director) above him or her when your business is a £5m-turnover business.

Team members want the feeling of progress – but have they deserved it? Well, yes, if they have hit their key performance indicators (KPIs, as they are sometimes abbreviated; we look at these in more depth in Rule 15 and 42). Then you can set them bigger, more challenging KPIs. Otherwise, it's definitely something to be avoided.

And even if they have hit their KPIs, it's not a particularly great reward. So, devise a mechanism for recognising those who hit their KPIs, such as a bonus, or a team-member-of-the-month award – not a fixed and permanent mechanism or job title that panders to egos and gives a false sense of authority. That helps no one, least of all your team member.

A better approach for delineating responsibilities would be, for example, to allow someone's business card to say "In charge of technical developments", rather than 'chief development officer. It is an accurate but not unalterable description of their role, rather than a permanent job title.

So don't give everyone big job titles. And if you can't agree on a job title, let them have the name 'consultant'.

No more and no less.

The days of job titles come from traditional hierarchical business, which operated in fixed structures. This is not how business is done today; today it needs to be highly adaptable and we all have to be willing to switch roles, to innovate at the drop of a hat, and responsibilities need to be flexible – especially if you are building a business that expects to see massive growth.

Only legally registered directors get the director job title

Please take extra care when giving someone the job title of 'director'.

Even though they may not have a place at your board meetings, an outside supplier may be excused for thinking that someone with a 'director' title does. Therefore, it is customary to expect directors to have some rights concerning signing contracts and taking on liabilities. If you do not wish other members of staff to have these rights, then don't give them job titles with 'director' in the name.

By the way, you don't want to give this contract-signing right to others, unless you are absolutely certain (see section 'Never delegate the contract signing', Rule 78).

37.

Pay recruitment fees on 'success'

A successful recruit for your business is someone who works out over a two- to three-year period. A successful recruit for an employment agency is someone who manages to get through the first three months without getting fired (as this is normally the limit to the recruitment agency's refund policy).

Are your interests aligned? Absolutely not!

Hence, a better way to use recruitment agencies is to take staff on fixed contracts and pay the recruitment agency a percentage of the salary that is due to the contractor. This is a common arrangement and can be placed via third-party umbrella companies (see Rule 27). It means that when you stop paying the contractor, you stop paying the agency.

This is a far better alignment of interests. It should ensure that your agency will work hard to find staff who will stick with you for six months or six years, because they will earn progressively more money in the process. This is opposed to anyone who can earn the agency a quick fee to help them achieve their monthly sales figures, but who could then disappear from your employ shortly thereafter.

And, although you may think it costs you more to hire like this – because you are paying a monthly percentage – it actually costs you less because you don't have the expense of firing and rehiring and the huge waste of management effort.

Just think – it costs two months' salary in recruitment fees alone to hire someone and typically one month's salary to fire them. So for every mistake you pay 25% of an annual salary.

Would you be willing to swap this for the equivalent of 10% per year? You should be.

38.

Keep new roles temporary

Establish all new roles as temporary, with fixed end dates. The default then is that the role will cease on that date unless the business takes a clear decision to make it permanent.

This forces an employee's mind to focus on that point and to deliver sufficient results to justify a new contract or extension.

Then you must be firm in insisting on clear evidence that the role should be extended. Make it clear from the beginning that you will need hard evidence of sales and profit and not promises of what might come next month.

Be very, very, very careful with recruitment decisions

The point that entrepreneurs miss is that recruitment is not an easily reversible process.

It is easy and fun to hire – albeit quite expensive. It is emotionally soul-destroying and exhausting to deal with and fire underperforming staff.

The way up is easy compared to the way down.

Therefore, you must recruit well. You must do everything in your power to get the right person in the right job. And you must be willing to slow your business growth down if you are unable to hire the right people.

And lastly, if it is not working, if your stress levels are too high, cut the business down in size and lay off those managers who are not delivering steady stable growth without your intervention.

If you are unsure in anyway, take them on a contract-only basis with a fixed end date. Or just hire freelancers instead.

39.

Quality team equals low stress levels

It is a common mistake for growth-driven entrepreneurs to allow their business to grow faster than their teams can handle. This will result in two things.

Firstly, a very high level of stress for the entrepreneur, who will have to patch and make up for the ensuing weaknesses or oversights in his or her team.

Secondly, you are likely not simply to weaken a team but to build a weak team in the first place. And if you build a weak team, this will slowly destroy your business or require you to spend considerably more effort trying to get the team to perform, training them, and then laying off weak members and trying to recruit again.

You'll exhaust yourself in the process and the business may well fail.

If you become too stressed, then you have the wrong team.

So take a long good hard look at your stress levels and then at your team and start to look for the right kind of talent that will enable you to move forward with much lower levels of stress.

40.

When staff leave, let them go without a fight

Staff leave. Don't fight it.

Staff will try to set up similar and competing businesses – wish them well, then carry on doing what your business does best. If you are as good as you say you are, then there is nothing to fear.

Sometimes staff get worn out or burnt out and need a change, just as you do. It is not personal; don't let it steal your peace.

Staff, too, sometimes just need to leave.

When someone does decide to leave, then it is a free opportunity to organise the business differently. Not least because it is very likely that the skills required by the job will have changed and you probably haven't noticed. This is certainly true if the business has grown.

Clients are amazingly receptive to new staff and new teams. It is almost as if when the staff member tires, then so too do your clients – everyone benefits from a fresh start.

I have often made the mistake of resisting when good people have expressed a decision to leave. Instead, I have now learned that it is better to let them leave and see what they have truly left behind. In the meantime, it is often unwise to immediately recruit their replacement, but see how the business runs without them for a few weeks and look to find different sets of skills to bring into the business if appropriate.

Never offer to raise the salary to keep staff

Offering to increase the pay of a member staff just to keep them is a dangerous act. It simply highlights to the remaining team that if they want a pay rise they must go out and get a new job offer.

You don't want to send this message. A pay rise to deter a departure is only recommended if the person leaving has been underpaid all along – in which case it is time to pay them fairly. Ideally, you'd get the pay levels right earlier on, but sometimes mistakes happen.

If you decide that the pay across your business is too low, then do something about it and thank the leaving employee for bringing it to your attention.

41.

Commit to excellence – fire the 'good'

Businesses all claim to be committed to 'excellence'. This commitment typically turns up in the business vision as well as the mission statement.

A commitment to excellence really means an intolerance of 'good'. So, following through on a commitment to excellence means some tough decisions.

Work with your team to help them to focus on excellence and accept that some (possibly many) won't make it and will need to be let go or moved onto other roles at which they can excel.

However, in a small business it is likely that you won't have enough roles to allow you to move your team around a great deal.

Therefore, if you find that a team member is excellent at only one or two aspects of their role, make their role part time and find someone else to deliver the rest. If you recruited them on a contract or freelance basis, this will be easy to implement.

In my previous business we found it very hard to persuade managers to let go good people in the search for excellence. The resistance, which was understandable, was based on the fear that the replacement would cost time and money to find and might prove worse.

From this fear, a willingness to accept 'good' becomes established. Therefore, think long and hard about whether you truly are committed to excellence, and, if you are, be willing to act.

Don't send ducks to eagle school

The alternative to letting people go because of underperformance is to set up training and support – often in-house training. However, you put yourself at risk of wanting the training for your underperforming team more than they actually want to be trained.

Again, this comes back to the level of desire.

If the individual is hungry and wants/asks for the training, then it is probably an investment worth making. If they don't ask, then it probably isn't worth training them anyway. Okay, some of your staff may be timid and not want to speak up, so make sure you have regular private conversations with them. And if they can't raise key questions about training with you in a private meeting, then it is unlikely that they really want the training enough to benefit from it.

The point here is that the request for training must come from the staff. Or even if you offer to fund training, you must then leave your staff to go and find the courses to support their training.

Too often you see companies forcing underperforming staff to get training – surely it is easier and quicker to find them a suitable role or show them the door and let them find a role elsewhere that suits their talents and interests?

At all times, you must avoid sending underperforming ducks to eagle school – some people just aren't cut out for delivering that certain roles with excellence, and no amount of training will help.

Don't fall for the 'teach a man to fish' fallacy

"Give a man a fish and you feed him for a day; teach a man to fish and you feed him for a lifetime."

So says the classic proverb. But for business training, it's a myth. The problem is that the employee will only fish they are hungry (see Rule 31).

If they are not hungry, then the training and knowledge may have been passed to them but they may not do anything with it.

And what if he or she, so to speak, just prefers the taste of beef anyway? The message for entrepreneurs here is that teaching a man to fish only works if he is:

- hungry

- likes fish

- wants to lean how to fish.

So don't waste your time or training on people who don't want it.

The Peter Principle

The Peter Principle states that: "In a hierarchy every employee tends to rise to their level of incompetence". In other words, so long as they are competent they are promoted. In due course, they reach a point at which they are no longer competent; and there they stay, no longer receiving promotions, and with others around them who have not yet reached their level of incompetence undertaking most of the work.

Now, partly this will already have been dealt with in the Rules on job titles, acting-up and splitting roles: you should have a team much less prone to this problem if you follow the advice there.

However, the problem will almost certainly occur from time to time all the same, and there is only one way to root it out – by establishing an easy way to end employment contracts.

The key issue with promoting from within is that employment rights built up over, say, five years at a £20k starter salary, become massive if that person is then promoted to £50k – the redundancy rights relate to their most recent pay, even though they didn't earn that amount for five years.

This method massively increases your business liabilities when you promote from within, and therefore undermines your business agility and ability to restructure should your market, teams or customers demand it.

That is why you should promote internal team members on a temporary basis only. (See Rule 38.)

42.

Measure team performance

People – contractors, freelancers, agencies and staff – are going to be your biggest cost and also your greatest opportunity.

Behind every great business there is a great team and that team gets fashioned and developed by constant attention. You now know what you have to do when it comes to hiring and firing. Let's turn to ways of managing and developing that team.

When your business grows and most of the frontline staff report to your managers, how will you know if your manager is any good or not? The answer is that how your manager delivers the KPIs of his or her team, and manages his or her team appraisals, will be your best indicator of managerial excellence or weakness.

What is an appraisal and a KPI?

All appraisals are based on a measurement – both quantitative and qualitative (i.e. based on numerical as well as individual evidence) – of a member of the team's ability to achieve certain specific goals. These measurements are made against their KPIs, or key performance indicators.

Typically a member of a team will have three KPIs. If they are senior they might also have another three on top (six in total) – but the first three will be the most important, and the second set will only be subsidiary.

It might be hard, initially, setting just three KPIs (you'll want a lot more) but greater focus will bring greater success – so keep reducing the list of 'important things' you have in mind until you have defined the three truly critical things that this person must deliver. Often this is best done in conjunction with your team member, as they will have a good idea about what is essential in their role.

An appraisal is simply a formal way of assessing whether your team member is delivering the agreed KPIs or not. A formal way means that you use a template questionnaire to review the goals, review the performance and set new goals.

The notes are written down and agreed on by both parties. These notes are then stored until you conduct the next performance review or appraisal.

Given this process, it is important to set out a clear template and clear set of (ideally) three measurable KPIs which can be quickly and easily assessed.

Never skip staff or team appraisals

Team member appraisals are very important even if your team is made up of regular freelancers and contractors. Essentially it is a way of checking whether you have the right person in the right role and whether they still have the right level of desire to do the job with excellence.

Appraisals are also hard work if the team members are not effectively managed and don't have KPIs. However, appraisals are a lot easier with freelancers because you will, more often than not, have already established the KPIs as a part of the contract between you.

Insist on regular appraisals to ensure that your managers stick to the agreed KPIs, and make sure that this is part of the contract. If a manager later complains that he or she doesn't have enough time to deliver the appraisals then this will be because there is a failure in the management of the team.

There is no reason why appraisals can't be run on a monthly basis – after all, if you pay a bill monthly (salary for instance) then you would want to know that you received what the supplier promised, right? So why treat your staff costs any differently? Staff are suppliers, just like the freelancer, agencies or traditional suppliers you contract with.

Remember that your appraisal is based around three key measurables – it is not a long things-to-do list. Ensuring that your managers keep the appraisals simple will mean that your teams have maximum freedom. So long as they are hitting the performance indicators, you can allow them to innovate in how they get there!

Now, if your manager delivers weak (or missed) appraisals in which key issues are not dealt with, it might be an idea to personally sit in on the next round of appraisals. You'll quickly find out if your manager is able to spot, raise and deal with the key issues. If not, you have the wrong manager in place.

In some cases you may choose to opt for three-monthly appraisals, when the work is less innovative and more systematic. This still gives sufficient opportunity to adapt the KPIs to a changing business environment. It also forces your managers to become effective at regularly setting and re-setting the agenda and re-focusing their teams.

If you skip KPIs and appraisals, or allow them to be skipped because you are 'busy', then you will be doing your managers no favours – they will relax their management standards (without their own KPIs and appraisals, they may do so without even being aware of it) and the quality of the output of your business will start to fall.

...unless you cancel all appraisals and replace with a simple measure

I have seen some businesses use a single, universal measure of success – revenue, for instance – with this becoming the weekly focal point for performance discussion. With this in place, you may consider that there is no need to run appraisals as the revenue figures tell you everything you need to know. Whether or not this is a sufficient measurement will, of course, come down to your own personal judgement about your business.

43.

Three months never says it all

Your team member may have the right skills and may be positive and helpful, but have they lost their sparkle? Have they lost their desire or hunger to succeed? If so, they are not the person they were three or six months ago.

This happens more often than we like to think. And it matters a great deal in an entrepreneurial and fast-growing business.

A perfectly good member of the team can turn into a poor performer for no reason other than they just don't want to do the job anymore.

Because, as business leaders, we are so programmed to expect to test a person in the interview and then in the first three months of a job, we forget that the greatest team members can burn out or get bored – and perhaps not long after this. Therefore, when this happens, we are surprised by the outcome and are slow to act – if we act at all. The fact is, three months never says it all.

Don't be slow. Just prepare yourself by understanding that this can always happen and that in a young cash-strapped business you don't have room for people who don't have the fire or excitement anymore.

44.

Managers and recruitment

Managers should spot roles that don't exist anymore

Essentially, if any role no longer has three clear KPIs then the position probably doesn't exist anymore and should be ended.

If the KPIs show that there are clear business needs and that they are not being met, then either the job is too senior for the people you have; your business processes are broken or need extending; or the person is no longer motivated to do the job.

This happens all the time. The important point is that the manager running the appraisal should be able to explain which of these three factors apply and be willing to do something concrete about it. Your manager should be proposing what to do without you having to ask. If not, the problem lies with your manager.

Managers manage team performance – not HR

Sometimes managers may say or encourage you to think that the solution to underperformance is that you need to hire a human resources (HR) manager or training specialist.

This is simply another excuse. The manager should be able to train the team to an acceptable level of skill. Yes, if further skill is needed, then training will help or training can form a part of a positive increase in productivity and skills, but it is not an excuse for non-performance.

Again, if your manager is skilled in that role then you would expect him or her to come forward with the training proposal. But just make sure that this is a proposal that arises from the team members (see Rule 41) or else you might just be sending ducks to eagle school.

Managers cannot shift business objectives due to trading conditions

Board meetings or management meetings (depending on what you need) will be about reviewing business performance, so whenever performance is below what was expected the question of, "Do we shift the objective or the manager?" will come up.

The answer to shifting objectives needs to be a clear and unequivocal answer – no!

That's it, really. It is a mistake to allow the business objectives to shift, as this allows more shifts next month, and so on – till the whole exercise becomes worthless.

You may choose to offer a stay of execution on the implementation of any consequences. However, ultimately you need to act on any failure to achieve the objectives, or else deliberately tear up the objectives and start again.

Allowing a shift simply encourages further shifts until your objectives are worthless and discredited.

45.

Making the KPIs solid

For some reason we find it easier to think in threes. 1, 2, 3 and A, B, C... Any important ideas around a job role, a contract or an agency brief, therefore, need to be summarised into three ideas and objectives.

That is why we must stick to three principal KPIs. Yes, you can have other objectives, but they are subsidiary.

Make sure you pick the right three KPIs to focus on for any given role; your business depends on it.

Remember that three KPIs mean your appraisal system remains simple and easy to measure and implement. This is very important if you intend to hold your managers to account through their ability to manage performance.

Make the KPI objectives measurable

This is the critical failing of some KPIs – their objectives are too loosely defined, and entail too much arguing over whether they've been met or not. It wastes time and invites a constant shifting of the boundaries.

What you need to decide (and we often fail to do) are two things:

1. who will record the objectives

2. what the consequences are if the objectives are not met.

Then, be prepared to measure the success or otherwise of the objectives; and secondly, be prepared to act if the objectives are not met.

If you cannot get agreement on the objectives, then see the earlier section in Rule 44 entitled 'Managers should spot roles that don't exist anymore'. Remember, if you don't have three clear, measurable KPIs, then the role doesn't exist. So, if no agreement can be reached, then get rid of the role.

What are three good personal objectives/KPIs?

For managers these will be:

- all staff achieve their KPIs (i.e. they have to manage their staff effectively)

- revenue objectives achieved (this might be a factor of their team's staff costs – for example, '4.5 times staff costs' – will ensure that the revenues keep the business profitable relative to its changing cost base)

- brand objectives achieved (a stronger brand or franchise will show an increase in revenue per employee/full-time freelancer and/or an increased profit margin).

For senior managers with profit and loss responsibility, you would expect to replace the 'revenue' objective with the 'profit' or 'profit margin' objective.

Take responsibility away from staff if performance is not right

If you are going to take key responsibilities away from underperforming staff members then you need to be able to give them to other members of staff or hire freelancers/contractors or outsource to an agency.

To be able to effectively follow up on your willingness to remove responsibility if a job is not performed to the required level (excellence), you need to:

- know or trust a manager to know the capabilities of each member of their staff in detail

- know freelancers and contractors who can replace those skills at short notice

- know the local agencies, firms of accountants, sales teams, marketing agencies, IT development companies etc… to whom you can outsource work.

Only external factors count as excuses

When making allowances for missed business objectives, only external factors count. It is too easy to make the mistake of allowing personal circumstances or 'unfortunate events' to cloud your judgement.

Okay, this is not black and white – but the point is that if the manager says "My staff are not up to the job," or "I lack the resources," then if the same manager agreed to the objectives previously, and agreed to the staff and resources, and has not resolved problems that arose, or even begun to resolve them, you simply have a failing manager who is making excuses.

The conclusion here has to be that the manager needs a different role or a different company.

46.

Poor performers get fired – not made redundant

A lawyer would never allow a business person to admit it, but it has become standard practice to disguise the firing of weak staff members by pretending that you are making the position redundant.

Okay, it is quicker to get rid of a member of staff who is not working out by use of redundancy than to work through their performance issues. However, it gives out the wrong message to those who remain and sets the wrong precedent.

Tempting though it may be at the time, the decision to let staff go via a fabricated redundancy process when they are underperforming sets a very dangerous standard. It is far better to work through the underperformance process and end up firing that member of staff.

This sounds unduly harsh, so why is this better?

Simply, you must be aware of the example that you are setting. If you establish in the mind of your remaining staff that underperformance is rewarded with a redundancy payment then you encourage underperforming staff to remain in your teams longer than they might otherwise do so.

It is far better, although harder work, to establish clear expectations in regards to performance and clear consequences for not meeting those expectations.

Don't be tempted to take the short cut; it is unlikely to help you in the long run.

And, once you've established the principle, you won't have to repeat it too often. Underperforming staff will just leave of their own free will.

47.

Deal with personnel problems immediately

Would you give them a job now? Would you give them a different job? If no, you need to act now.

There is no excuse for not acting quickly. It was Jack Welch, former chairman of General Electric (GE), who said that he had never made a decision to let someone go too quickly.

It is always a mistake to delay these decisions – for both you and, crucially, for the person concerned.

All sales staff excuses are equal

Salespeople are a critical part of any business. So when they promise to deliver revenue and fail at the last minute, what do you do?

"I am just closing that sale" …"give me a couple more days and I'll deliver it"…

Beware. This kind of response can sometimes be a marvellous display not of the truth but of the salesperson's skill at negotiation and smooth talking – abilities they should have been more diligently directing towards your objectives. The problem isn't so much that they're failing to deliver – even the best miss targets – it's that they're not being honest with you and frank about it, and have been forced, therefore, to devote their (doubtlessly considerable) sales talents to selling you reasons not to worry, rather than selling your customers your product. If they're experienced salespeople, this is bad practice. And they should know it.

You are wise not to listen too much to their "'next month's sales" projections at this point. Instead, start to use sales figures midway through the month as your best prediction to sales at the end of the month. If you reach the end of the month and the gap hasn't been made up, then you've got to take stronger action.

Many entrepreneurs are from a sales background, and will find this quite natural. However, if like me you are not from a sales background, you'll need to overcome this classic error pretty quickly if you are going succeed in an entrepreneurial business.

Strike one, strike two, strike three and out

As the entrepreneur of a growing business, you have to pass on responsibility. When someone else picks up that responsibility, they need to both be held accountable and also perform. Okay, so they don't have your experience. Well, they can ask your advice.

But it is critical that from day one of passing the responsibility to them you make it clear that this is a temporary trial, and that you operate a 'three strikes and out' policy.

This policy means you give them two chances to get it wrong before they must put right both of those errors and not repeat it again. If they make the same error a third time, then take the responsibility away (depending on the situation, that might mean you are letting them go).

48.

Use great questions to tease out performance

Asking a salesperson, "Have you made any sales yet?" sounds desperate and is demotivating. So how do you get to the performance without alienating or demoralising half your team?

Try these questions:

- What is the best thing you've done today?

- What is the best result you've had this week?

- Who is this week's favourite client?

- Who is going to win the team prize?

Why are these great questions? Because you are asking them in public and you want to find something good to praise. If you find that performance is poor or not fruitful, then draw them into a separate office and deal with it privately.

When there, don't ask, "Did you make any sales today?" but rather say "Tell me about your best pitches today… "

Most offices today are open plan and therefore questions need to be asked in the positive with the expectation that you'll get a positive reply.

49.

Promote anyone who makes their job redundant

A key way to encourage good behaviour is to only promote those people who have made their previous job redundant. That is, they have improved the processes so much, there is no longer much work left for them to do. This person deserves more responsibility within your organisation.

Yes, that is right, you want to encourage people to make their job redundant. You want people to NOT hang onto their job, but see that the way to career advancement is via getting rid of the need for their current job.

This will help make your business truly innovative and highly entrepreneurial.

50.

100% management support – all the time

Machiavelli saw this most clearly. He stated that people – and for entrepreneurs that's clients, freelancers, team members, suppliers, competitors – are either *for* you or *against* you.

Particularly among senior managers, someone who is not able to back up the CEO may wish to protect their position by adopting the apparently reasonable 'not for you, not against you, but neutral' position. It is a grievous mistake to allow this.

This is actually a senior manager invariably taking a position against the CEO but playing politics with their unwillingness to declare their opposition. The manager may also be attempting to remain in the flow of information simply so that they can strengthen their own position. It is a cowardly stance for any manager to take. Your role is to flush it out into either clearly stated opposition or clearly stated support.

And, if the manager moves to a position of support, look to their actions to see that what they do matches their words. Set some clear and specific tasks and objectives related to this.

However, it is most likely that neutral support will convert into opposition – and that is why it is best treated as such. It would be a wise step to remove this person from key meetings, business decisions or business information until they are able to make up their mind.

51.

Know employees by their fruits

If you have ever worked in a white-collar industry then you will have been surrounded by people who got hired not because they could wield a hammer or lift a ton of hay, but because they were good talkers.

The modern recruitment process is a test of a person's ability to talk and persuade you that they know what they are doing, rather than a person's ability to do the job. Don't forget that research tells us that we only succeed in hiring the best person 14% of the time by interview alone, so we shouldn't be surprised by the danger (and cost) of falling for the smooth talk.

Look around your organisation to find the people who are really doing the work. They are the ones to value. At the end of the day, all of us, our team members included, will be known not for what we said, but what we did.

If the business runs out of cash, then words won't count any more.

52.

Do away with formal meetings

To get the focus on fruit – not words – put an end to meetings around a table with comfortable chairs and instead stand at the workstation and ask questions.

On the job, plus live questions, is the way to find out who is delivering what.

The simplest way to promote this practice is to close half the meeting rooms or not have them in the first place.

53.

The team is the hero

Often, entrepreneurs end up looking for a hero. If someone in your team is pretty good, you'll make them into a hero because you are just so glad that they are on board and at last you can hand over some of the responsibility.

You know what I'm going to say? Yep, this is a mistake.

The hero in the business is never a single person, but the team. No single person can make or break a company; it is what happens to the teams that count.

It takes time and patience to find the right people, to replace those that fall by the wayside and to build a team and keep that team moving in the right direction. Looking for single heroes devalues teamwork and the team ethic and is likely to annoy more people than it encourages.

Let the team choose individual awards

If you wish to give individual awards – say, for best team members – then let the teams themselves choose the winners. Don't let management have any say at all.

This way, you respect the team's views and wishes and the team feels valued by the managers. You are beginning to treat the team with the respect it deserves – and needs – if it is going to flourish.

54.

Have a wise head on hand

Young companies feel the need to share the business with new partners or staff.

This makes sense if managed carefully, but generally when the business is new – and especially if the entrepreneur is young – there is a risk of naivety. Any equity or profit agreement can be too broad and not based around delivery of results.

A worse mistake is to hand out equity or share options to anyone and everyone, just for being there.

One solution to this indiscretion is to keep an older, wiser head – a chairperson – on hand, who can say 'no' to some of the things that you might find hard to turn down. This will work well if you are willing to listen to them.

It also allows you to say, "I'd love to – but my chairperson says no". For some reason, people find this easier to swallow and you'll end up making fewer enemies.

55.

Reward long-term value creation

Whether you take on a contractor or a full-time employee (you already know my advice about this, but hey, you might still have legacy employees) you should include a bonus element.

A bonus element should match the KPIs that you set out in your team member's performance or appraisal review *and* be pegged to long-term value creation within your business.

However, it is worth repeating that the nature of a contractor or freelancer is that they will see continuing work or recommendations/introductions for other work as a bonus in itself.

Obviously, full-time employees don't see repeat work (or keeping their jobs) as a benefit, which is, again, why freelancers and contractors are so much more appreciative of what you do and therefore often easier to work with.

So, to be clear, a bonus doesn't have to be a cash bonus. There are many ways to reward great work and commitment; money is just one of those!

The employee is much harder to motivate and reward and you need to start building bonus structures which work (i.e. rewarding for the right results but without being too complex).

Don't have long-term contractual bonus commitments

It is natural for staff or team members to want long-term commitments to bonus structures, but you should and must avoid this.

The kind of bonus that works now, for your business in its current state, may not work in one or three or five years' time. The market you operate in, the macroeconomic environment, the size of your business and your team's make up, could all have radically changed in this time. Hence, your bonus structure needs to be able to change too.

You must make this absolutely clear to all team members at the outset of their employment with you so that, if the structure changes, you don't create disappointment and resentment.

The maximum length of any bonus or commission structure must be to the end of the year (calender or tax), at which point you reserve the right to alter, remove or replace the structure. Make sure you state clearly and openly that any bonus structure has a definitive end date and might not be renewed or replaced.

Finding a business-value basis for the bonus

Entrepreneurs who are new to bonuses and human behaviour often pick the wrong basis for working out the bonus and therefore get unexpected behaviour. Typically, young entrepreneurs will choose revenue or sales as the bonus basis and this can dangerously encourage a sales team to make weak or phantom sales just to reach the target.

The best way to construct a bonus is to figure out what the business would regard as an excellent result and then work backwards. If you can't work out what is an excellent result, then don't run a bonus scheme until it becomes clear.

Remember, an excellent result is a growth of profit margin and sustainability, as we saw in earlier Rules.

No bonus should ever create a situation where a staff member wins but the company loses. This is where you find that you are paying for the individual to do something that either has no business benefit or is detrimental to the business.

An example of a detrimental bonus might be to reward someone based on a project finishing early – which sounds great, but perhaps the project finished early because the specifications changed and were simplified? What's actually being rewarded here, then? More worryingly, a staff member might rush a job to finish a project early and earn their bonus for less-than-excellent work.

Better forms of bonus include rewarding team members not solely for prompt delivery of a technical project, but based on the length of its testing and acceptance phase (if it is short).

Another example would be rewarding a staff member who wins repeat business, rather than just single instances of business. This can kick in when a customer buys for a second time, and ensures that the bonus reward is for delivering high quality customers – adding to your long-term company worth.

Unlimited bonus structures only for pure sales businesses

This is a point which is really only applicable to sales staff – and ought not to be attempted for salespeople in a business where they are less than 80 or 90% of the workforce. It will only breed justified resentment amongst those whose jobs don't allow them to fulfil the metric you set.

It is, in short, unlimited bonuses based on weekly or monthly ability to generate sales – specifically, repeat sales. Indeed, I would set it in the employee contract as: "The salesperson earns 1% of any revenue from repeat customers."

The salesperson's focus thus shifts onto winning repeat business – and then maintaining the repeat business. This structure will take longer to build a large bonus pool, but it will reward a more sustained effort. And it will ensure that your business is focused on repeat business, which is great for you.

The reason this works is that a few high earners will motivate your lower earners much more than an even spread of pay and reward – so long as they know that they, too, can attain the higher pay (and you really have arranged your reward structures so that they can). It may sound perverse, but your sales team will be more motivated by seeing an individual earn four times their own annual salary for outstanding performance, than if that same cash was spread equally among the whole team.

This is not to encourage you to overpay some team members and underpay others. What this is, if devised and publicised correctly, is a flexible and helpful tool for getting the most out of your sales team. Reward key individuals for outstanding performance and make sure that the rewards only continue if the performance continues and that all staff can see how they can achieve this higher level.

This is the benefit of a bonus structure which is unlimited – it allows a few individuals to earn a lot of money and this will be an incentive for other staff who want to earn more money, too.

However, such bonus structures typically require rapid payment of the bonus – as this allows all your team to believe that they have an equal chance to succeed – and therefore has the danger that your bonus will be based on a simple measure of revenue, which puts it at risk of gaming, typically declaring sales before they are actually secured or offering a customer a discount which has not been approved if they book before a certain deadline.

When to use profit, when revenue for bonuses

Any business which is facing a reducing profit margin is in trouble, which is why profit is a more preferable basis for a bonus than revenue – for the business, at least. However, it is impossible to calculate the profit on a monthly basis and therefore this is not an effective basis for a bonus for frontline salespeople. It just won't motivate them.

Instead, it is better to keep the team rewarded on sales but the *sales manager* rewarded on both monthly sales and quarterly profit. If the sales manager has an opportunity for a large profit-based bonus over a longer term then he or she will be the one to look after the salespeoples' margins and manage their expenses and costs.

This effectively puts the responsibility for revenue in the hands of the frontline sales staff, and the profit focus in the hands of the manager. By virtue of the bonus you have made one responsible for revenue and the other responsible for profit. This is a good structure to use, but of course you will need to make sure that you are willing to hand over profit responsibility to your manager. Can they handle it?

Lastly, if you are unable or unwilling to give profit responsibility to a senior manager (or let's say you need to take back the responsibility due to failure) then it is important that you recognise that the profit responsibility lies with you – and not your team.

Your team will constantly push up costs and reduce margin (possibly by heavy discounting) and you will need to be vigilant to ensure that a balance is kept and the margin remains intact. One way to do this is to only allow sales that are at least 90% (or some other agreed figure) of list price to count in overall sales figures. So, if the salesperson requests a discount of more than 10% then it can be accepted on the understanding that it won't count towards the salesperson's target. This mechanism will reduce the discounting quickly.

Equally, you might have a cap on the expenses of travelling salespeople – after which any excess is taken from the bonus.

Only salespeople get individual revenue bonuses

Some bonuses are based solely on individual performance. These can only be commission for salespeople. This is the most effective way to stimulate the frontline sales team.

Equally, it allows the sales manager to keep a simple list of revenue performance by salesperson and reward the person who is at the top of the list each month. This is a powerful motivation for all salespeople.

It also allows the salespeople to compare and measure themselves against each other. This is an important point. Great salespeople are naturally competitive and will want to be at the top of the leader board. So publish a sales board with names and amounts sold. It is a classic mistake to establish the bonus structure and agree the commissions but then fail to communicate this and publicly reward it.

Non-sales people must have team bonuses

However, as you move away from roles that have a direct and immediate revenue impact, individual bonuses can become meaningless and distracting. This happens when it is not clear to the person how they might influence the achievement of a bonus.

At this point, it is time to stop using individual bonuses. Instead, your bonus needs to reflect the success of the team, as this will encourage collaborative working.

You will also find that the bonus can only make up a smaller part of the overall package.

Again, a key benefit for contract and freelance staff is that they get more work or receive positive referrals and this is an important hidden bonus.

Bonus can be team of teams

Team bonuses help to pull the team together. This is particularly helpful when you have teams that are pulling apart from each other. It can be used to address a particular problem or it can become a central part of everyone's pay.

You can also give to competing or warring teams the same bonus structure and goals in order to force them to depend on each other and so bring them together.

Such a multi-team bonus is clearly going to be based on either divisional or company-wide performance, which has another benefit...

The John Lewis example of company-wide bonuses

Some companies, such as the John Lewis Partnership, have created unique methods of sharing profit with all staff. This method works well for John Lewis because it has been a founding principle of the company, and over many years, and with much effort, its existence and benefits have been communicated thoroughly to all partners.

Over time, such a commitment will have tremendous power with your teams – not least in that it will mark your business out as different from alternative employers.

However, young businesses may not get off the ground before this kind of bonus structure settles in – and therefore it is unlikely to be appropriate in the early pre-profit stages unless you choose to make staff / team involvement a key principle of your business and that has all sorts of new risks associated with it, such as a lack of control in the entrepreneur's hands.

56.

Be wary of bonuses?

There is, however, another view: bonuses don't work and have no place in business. If your business commitment is to excellence, then you simply manage the performance of the individuals closely and part company quickly if the performance is not up to scratch.

In the ideal world this is the perfect solution, but for it to be effective you need to have the facility to quickly and easily let your staff go. Again, this would point to the freelance and contract staff structure, or at least a structure in which you can fire staff without significant complexity or cost.

In such cases, you can simply agree the fee for the work. And pay top rates.

My view is that, in the early stages of a business, this simple non-bonus approach is the best. However, the error that many entrepreneurs have made, myself included, is that what suits a business at one stage will not suit it at a later stage. Never forget this.

57.

Use profit-share bonuses

Using profit as the basis of bonuses is hard to manage as it requires the explanation of your accounts in some detail to all members of your team and some just won't understand this or trust the calculations. So the value of this kind of bonus depends on the kind of team that you have.

If you are predominately a white-collar business with team members that are highly educated, then this wider knowledge is a good thing and the use of profit as a basis for bonuses is generally a good idea, unless your team is entirely cynical. If you have a high proportion of mechanics working machines, then it is less likely that they will feel much personal connection with a profit-based bonus.

The key point is that, as any individual's ability to influence the company-wide profit is limited, the relative size of this bonus to the overall package therefore needs to be modest.

The great thing about profit-share schemes is that they help build the sale value of the business (as a business's value is a measure of its current and future profitability) whilst not costing anything up-front.

Now, there still remains a question about whether it is worth giving away hard-earned profit. Will this just be sharing a windfall or will the bonus structure ensure that greater effort and success are fairly rewarded? Remember, sharing profit with team members is about giving cash that is due to shareholders to employees instead. Why would shareholders agree to this?

Shareholders will agree if the bonus drives forward the profit generation of the business, which in turn, of course, increases the value of the business. Hence the payback is that shareholders would expect a higher sale value in the medium term.

Now, remembering that shareholders are actually interested in profit margin, if you can tie the bonus to profit margin then you are tying together the interests of shareholders, staff and business much more closely.

Lastly, shareholders might be more easily persuaded to share profits if they are based on an increase in profit (or profit margin).

Now, a bonus based on increase in profit margin will be even harder to communicate, but once a payout is made, you'll galvanise the teams in your business to stretch for another bonus next year – and, suddenly, you'll get a much greater engagement with the idea of how to increase profit margins.

58.

Pay out some profits as dividends for directors

A bonus structure that is based on a percentage of the shareholder dividend has lots of benefits – it creates a very inclusive atmosphere around the business and will benefit those team members who choose to stay with the company a long time.

However, it is no longer clear that long-term or career employees are quite the value that they were once thought to be, and they are unlikely to form part of a growth entrepreneurial company.

So, to make this work in the 'here and now' of modern business life, the business needs to make a commitment to pay out a minimum share of its profits as dividends – perhaps 25% or 35%. This way, current senior staff can be sure that they will see some benefit of a bumper profit year – and that their benefits will be in proportion to those received by shareholders.

Bonus on increase-in-dividend payout

A neat way to encourage great business performance is to pay senior managers a per cent of the increase in dividend payout. Therefore, if dividend payouts increase by £200,000 then they might share 30% of that increase.

Of course, next year, the barrier for dividend profits is now £200,000 higher and, therefore, to earn the big bonus again, managers will need to grow the business more, maximising the value of the new cash available for dividends and reinvestment.

This method also negates the need to give senior managers shares or share options, as they are now connected to the true performance of the business – the rates of return (or dividends) to shareholders.

59.

Keep two accounts

Set up two business accounts with your bank. One account is for the day-to-day running of the business. The other account is for the investments that the business wishes to make.

Any manager who wishes to make the case for an investment can do so on the basis that only what is available in the investment account can be spent and that his or her idea needs to compete with any other idea to take this money. This structure can also help to manage your profit bonus.

A pre-agreement that a fixed percentage of cash (say 33%) will be placed in the investments account each year and the remaining 67% paid out to shareholders is a quick way to:

- solve the issue of profit bonuses – i.e. what is the size of the pool and who gets to decide it?

- show that reinvestment is available for the business to grow as a whole, which will help drive profitability in future years.

Of course, the board of directors reserves the right to change the allocations when the business is under considerable pressure, but any change should be on a temporary basis such that it defaults back to the norm when markets stabilise.

60.

Pride goes before a fall

Puffed-up pride is a classic sign that a business is going to hit trouble and then fall rapidly from grace. My wife says that if you own shares in a company that moves from shabby buildings into a nice new shiny city-centre glass tower, you should sell all your shares immediately.

Pride before the fall is a grave danger for successful businesses. The telltale signs include expensive cars, unnecessary trips and costly 'training' regimes. Do you recall the AIG debacle of September 2008, in which the board members went on a multi-million-dollar brainstorming weekend (a golf outing) just days before the US government bailed it out for $85bn?

Even if you are not particularly prideful, after years of success you are likely to believe that anything you begin will succeed. So, in your second venture you may spend too much cash too fast. You may not be heedful of serious market pressure in your business until it is too late.

The advantage of an experience of a failed business is huge – it reminds you to stay humble and avoid such mistakes. You are more likely to perceive problems while you still have time to do something about them.

Obviously there is no point in setting out to fail deliberately, just for the valuable lessons – so should you be in this (dubiously?) fortunate situation of having experienced a failed business, do all that you can to avoid hubris. Pride is the ultimate form of carelessness. So be careful.

61.

Don't diversify to escape trouble

Typically if a business is in trouble it begins thinking about diversification – which sounds like a good idea, but actually, simply encourages trouble... In many ways, this is similar to a political leader who, running into trouble domestically, becomes interested in foreign policy; and then makes a hash of both.

Diversification is not the same as following shifts in the market. Instead it is the attempt to create brand new products in new markets where your teams don't have any real experience.

If a business is losing money, this is a very high-risk strategy because you need, firstly, to be right first time round about the needs and pricing power in the new market (you won't have the cash to attempt it a second time), and secondly, it all has to happen in a fixed time frame; namely, before the core business goes bust.

Hence, diversification can often be disastrous.

The other occasion when diversification does real damage to a business is when the core business has matured and the executives are looking around for more exciting things with which to occupy themselves. This tends to happen in large companies, but the source of the problem is the same – the desire to make the company big in volume, as this reflects well on the directors, with less attention paid to quality.

Remember, the measure of quality in your business is your profit margin. Therefore, if your diversification efforts are forecast to reduce your profit margin – even temporarily – they are probably a very bad idea. This is why a mature company is better to accept a shrinking market or no growth, and to concentrate on profit margin.

If profits are good, these can be paid out to shareholders and directors via profit bonuses. If those shareholders wish, they can take their money and invest in new businesses with separate legal structures – so that the performance of one company will not bring down the other company. In some cases, this can be managed within a group.

In the meantime, get back to your core business and reduce it to a level at which it has a strong profit margin. A business that is in trouble is better off spending its time reviewing its key managers to see why they are not delivering, than running after half-baked new ideas.

It might also be time to consider exiting your existing business if, on reflection, your desire for diversification is simply a symptom of your disbelief in its strengths.

New diversified businesses go into new legal entity

Almost regardless of how you choose to arrange your group, then, the new diversified product or service should be held in a new company. Doing this involves more set-up costs and therefore is only worth doing if the opportunity is strong enough. Indeed, helpfully, it will force you to really consider whether the opportunity is worth it, and to balance the risk and return against anything that might be done with the capital in your existing business.

Don't forget that you can also hand the cash back to the shareholders – should the shareholders not be of one mind about the new venture – and then only work with those who wish to invest in a new venture.

Either way, diversification is going to benefit from a new legal entity.

62.

Let go – faster

Young entrepreneurs make the classic mistake of not letting go because no one else can run the business or perform that activity better than they can. In such circumstances, it is time for a reality check.

If you are a true entrepreneur then you'll be good at an amazingly wide range of different things. You can probably sell or market your product. You'll be accustomed to networking and developing products and services. You'll understand opportunities and be able to spot niches.

You'll be good at all these – but you probably won't be great at any. And hanging on to too many roles is a major mistake.

Why?

Each of us becomes great at something through practice and constant trial and error – and if you deny that opportunity to others then you will be holding back your organisation. Once the business starts to grow, your role needs to change and you must move on. All future work will be delivered via other people (staff, freelance, agencies) and, therefore, instead of being an expert at doing, you need to become an expert at delivering through other people.

You can't avoid this if you are going to build a great business, so let go faster and learn about delegation quicker.

63.

Letting others have a go will help them develop greatness

Look back at yourself ten years ago. Are there some skills that you've gained that you didn't have then? How did you get those skills? And if you are now particularly strong in some areas, how did you get those skills?

Yes, you probably had an aptitude for marketing or sales or technology, but you gained your great skill set by having the freedom to try things out – and learning from trial and error.

Now, if you don't let go of exercising some of those skills you will never see your people develop the skills that you have, nor will you see them surpass you and become better than you. But that's exactly what you need them to do.

You have to let go, to allow others to grow. Of course, you will bite your nails when you see easy tasks get messed up, and that is why you need a strike one, strike two, strike three and out approach (see Rule 47).

64.

Eliminate puff

These days nearly every company claims in its mission statement to have a high level of 'integrity' and, no doubt, that it likes to cuddle furry animals too. This statement usually appears in the 'About Us' web page.

This is puff – and you need to purge your business of this rubbish.

It may be true that your business has high levels of integrity and is an ethical organisation, but overuse of these phrases has devalued them. So don't use them. Better still, if you know what these phrases mean for your business, then state it clearly. For instance, if they mean that 100% satisfaction is guaranteed through a range of quality control and returns policies, then it is better to say that – and to say concretely what they are.

This also means you'll only use claims that you can legitimately stand behind.

I was recently shown a business proposal for an enterprise that claimed to be an 'ethical service'. I searched the 64-page, densely written document and found 26 examples of use of the word 'ethical' – but in no place did it explain what this meant, nor how this service was different from, say, an unethical service. Later I was told that one of the principal backers for the business was the ex-porn king of Los Angeles. As you can imagine, I didn't bother trying to get a clear explanation of what 'ethical' meant to him.

So it is best to avoid the words 'integrity' or 'ethical', unless backed up with detail (and even then, I'd just have the detail), because usually they are meaningless – and people, increasingly, know it. There's no point in being in the company of porn kings.

Understand the difference between a business vision and mission statement

Aha! This is a trick – in my practical business experience there is no clear distinction between these two concepts; in many cases they are the same thing. The terms are so widely used as to not have any clear definition in usage, no matter what textbooks may say.

Do you need either or both? Well, yes, you need to know what your business is about and what it stands for (business vision) – and that message should be expressible (mission statement). So you need both, together, at the same time.

It may be appropriate to adjust the message for different audiences (investors, staff, clients, suppliers). In some cases a business vision is shared with staff and a mission statement is shared with clients – but it should be the same message in essence, albeit adapted for each individual audience.

65.

Build your brand

Your brand is much more than an image. It is best seen as a sum of all the relationships and feelings that people have towards your business or products. I use the word 'people' because we could be talking about customers, suppliers, staff or freelance talent pools. The other group to consider are your competitors, too.

Each of these might have a different relationship with your brand. Just because one is going well, it doesn't mean that there aren't adjustments you can make to improve another. So, Primark might have had a great brand for cheap fashionable clothing among its existing customers, but some of its potential customers associated the brand with exploitation through low wages. Primark addressed this by publishing information about working conditions in its factories and showing what it does to help people in poor countries. In some respects immaterial to those who were already happy to shop there, it was effective for those who weren't. Branding initiatives don't have to be universally targeted.

* * *

The key point about a brand is that it allows you to charge a premium. Compare a well-known brand-name cereal with a high-quality own label – probably not much difference in the quality of the product, but a higher price can be charged. And a few extra pennies might mean the brand earns double the profit.

So, recalling that your business is worth its profit (payable to shareholders) over time, then an increase in profit margin thanks to brand value increases the value of your business. So brands really do have a genuine and direct business value.

Also it is easy to forget the impact of your brand on suppliers – but don't! They also care about your brand, and the quality of your brand will help bring you favourable business terms. When I worked at the Economist Group – publishers of the eponymous magazine – suppliers always wanted to work with us because they wanted to be able to list *The Economist* as a customer. We were able to negotiate deals and get access to new media technology ahead of other groups, even though the business was relatively small for a global publishing business.

Therefore, treat brand investment as an investment in the long-term profitability of your business. It does have a critical place, and although it won't provide immediate revenue flow it will allow you to charge more for your products than would otherwise have been possible, as well as allowing you to get better deals from suppliers. Both are utterly key to a higher profit margin. You'll also find the best talent wanting to work for you.

66.

Protect your brand and IP

You have to protect your intellectual property by registering patents and trademarks, as well as by devising a strategy for fighting infringements.

There are two levels of infringement:

- small-scale – usually someone setting up a similar-sounding domain name

- large-scale – a direct attack on your business.

Small-scale infringements

The level of small-scale IP infringement is now massive – thanks largely to the internet. You therefore need a mechanical and efficient way of dealing with this. Ask a firm of lawyers to write a series of standard letters demanding that the infringers cease and desist (i.e. stop doing what they are doing). Keeping these general letters on hand, ready to be tailored and dispensed when necessary, allows your admin team or a freelance lawyer to spend one or two days a month efficiently protecting your brand, and in most cases minimising the damage of the infringements.

I once ran a very successful property investment website called Property Secrets and we had an infringement by a chap selling his book under the name *Property 'Investment' Secrets*. Clearly, he was attempting to pass himself off as our brand, and after a few letters he stopped the worst of his infringement and took care not to copy our brand in future websites. We didn't get the offending website domain removed from him, but we did manage to substantially curtail his activities and limit the brand damage he caused – all with a few standard letters.

Large-scale infringements

Large-scale infringements might include examples where an employee stole your customer database or someone copied your patented product design. In this case, the financial damage to your business could be substantial and on this basis you will need to rigorously defend your IP rights.

Essentially, any court will look to see the financial damage that has been caused by the people who are infringing your IP, and, if they find them guilty, they will award you losses to the level of damage that you claim.

Classic examples of this include the action by NTP, a US technology company, who claimed that the technology underpinning RIM's BlackBerry mobile phone belonged to them. After years of litigation, the case was settled for damages of US$612.5m.

The truth is that a successful company with a strong brand will draw a greater level of interest from fraudsters and those who wish to infringe your brand. Therefore, as you grow more successful you will need to work harder to defend your business. And the ability to defend the business will depend on how well you set up the trademarks and patents in the first place. So speak to your trademark lawyer before your business really takes off and once you know which brand names you want to put investment and effort behind (Rule 70 will help here).

67.

Product = brand = product = brand

Think of a piece of rope – it might be a long piece of rope. At one end you have your product or service, and at the other end you have your brand image/statement and description.

If they pull in different directions, you'll either go nowhere or the rope will snap.

And, even though brand is at one end and your product or service is at the other, it's all one piece of rope. So, set alight to your brand at one end, and the fire will quickly travel to the product and service. Soak the product and service end of the rope in water, and the damp will slowly pass to the brand.

These two – brand and product/service – are both indivisible and yet distinct at the same time. Never neglect one, thinking that the other will take care of things. The best product in the world will fail if its brand is unattractive; the coolest brand is useless if the product or service is poor.

68.

Establish clear ownership of code, content and process

Your business will generate new ideas, code for websites and proprietary technology, and a variety of business processes known legally as 'trade secrets'. At the same time, businesses increasingly use information and publishing (via blogs etc.) to communicate and share ideas with clients and suppliers.

So it is important that all that content belongs to your business – including the right to use any content contributed by other third parties who may not get paid for the right either. (For example, posts on forums you host and responses to your blogs or articles.)

It is important that you clearly establish rights to your intellectual property, and that although all such rights may allow a use appropriate for the task – so a freelancer can use your technical code to help them do their job – this does not infer that you have given them ongoing rights to use it.

69.

Own your clients

Who has the key relationship with your clients – your brand or your team members?

If the clients are loyal to your brand, then team members can come and go and clients will remain. If your client's loyalty to particular members of your staff is very much stronger than your business brand, then your clients will follow those staff should they leave.

This is the problem that high level services such as banking and legal services suffer from.

Obviously, in some respects, clients who value your team members is a good problem to have – it should mean your staff are performing out of their skins. But it could also mean that your brand is weaker than it ought to be. In either case, it requires some extra work on the brand side of things.

So, this might be where you engage a brand marketing agency, and look to establish a strong and distinctive brand which supports your team members and their relationships with their clients, but also makes it clear why the clients would wish to stay with the *firm* for the long term.

70.

Refocus your brand – regularly

Strong brands are often the result of doing something exceptionally well. It is likely that after a few years of entrepreneurial ducking and diving, and attempts to squeeze profit and margin out of your business model, you may have covered a lot of ground and your brand might mean a lot of different things to different people.

Don't panic. It doesn't mean that your business has a problem – all the really strong brands have gone through this. It is often just the time to get really clear, again, about what you are and what you are not. In fact, it's probably better to put energy into it at this stage, when you've found and developed your business's strengths, than foreshortening your horizons early on.

That way, as you now begin to increase your marketing spend on non-direct-revenue-generating marketing – i.e. brand marketing – you don't waste your money. And, as your brand becomes stronger in its niche, so it becomes harder for copycat companies to copy you (or simply too expensive for them to enter your market).

71.

Measure resolutions as well as complaints

Maintaining brand value amongst your customers is obviously key, and an important part of this is how you deal with complaints.

Working out how well you're doing this can be counterintuitive – there's actually a pretty big error that it's easy to slip into over time, and that's to automatically equate low numbers of complaints with a satisfied customer base and a well protected brand. Nope. Not necessarily.

The quantity of complaints will vary from business to business, but if you measure the resolution of complaints rather than the number of complaints, you'll have a far better measure for how your brand is likely to be doing.

It is better to have 20 complaints and 18 resolved, than to have four complaints and none resolved.

The first situation, 20 complaints, 18 resolved, suggests not only the obvious (that you are very good at resolving customer's problems), but the less obvious and equally important conclusion – although you've got some issues to address, you are good at encouraging your customers to tell you what they think, and they have faith in your ability to solve any problems they have. This means that they have a more intimate and respectful relationship with your company. That you have solved 18 also suggests that the remaining two will likely be solved shortly.

The second situation – four complaints, none resolved – suggests not only that you are not solving any customer complaints, but that, although their number appears to be small, you haven't a hope of starting to. It is therefore likely that, by now, far more than four customers have problems with you – it's just that they're so disenchanted they can't be bothered to get in touch. They'll let other people know about it, though, don't you worry! Website forums, fellow customers, family members and friends – and their friends in turn – will soon know every reason why they shouldn't have anything to do with your company.

Clearly, four complaints and four resolutions is the ideal! But, as you can now see, the important part of that is the number of resolutions.

72.

Rattle the cage to maintain excellence

The sign of a contented business is a profitable one.

If the profits are healthy (by whatever margin is appropriate for your business sector) then morale is likely to be good and relationships between the team members effective. However, this is where a mistake can creep in. Once content, the drive and push for excellence by your staff might turn out to be more theoretical than actual.

The skill then is not to rest on your laurels but push on to the next goal – whilst also keeping the justified and helpful contentment going.

Another way of putting it is this – your job as a business leader is to rattle the cage. But not to tip the whole thing over. You need to keep supplying your team with something to jerk them into action and keep them from complacency. Establishing and maintaining this balance will keep the focus on excellence at the heart of your successful and growing business.

I have seen very successful entrepreneurs turn up at the office unexpectedly throw a new business idea at the team and stay all week until it is launched. I've seen the same effect achieved by deciding to conduct a review of all roles and functions. Equally, it helps to rattle the cage by landing an unexpected piece of business with a tight delivery deadline.

There are many ways to rattle the cage, and each of us will do it in a slightly different way, but do it we must.

73.

Know your source of world-class business excellence

A business can only be excellent at something that you and your team love to do – so, for me, that is books, online media and marketing. It makes sense for me to start and run businesses which are in that sector. And it makes sense for you to start and run businesses in whatever area you are passionate about. (See Rule 5.)

Nevertheless, there are lots of mediocre media businesses out there, and you'll come across plenty of mediocre businesses in whatever sector you go into. I have even had a job in some of them in the past. So might you. They are not bad businesses. They are not incompetent, either. They are just run-of-the-mill; they just tick over. They are eminently vulnerable to copycats, and will never make much in the way of waves, although for now they make enough money to keep everyone happy. In some ways, this is quite an achievement, but in others, far from what you as an entrepreneur should be interested in. They're actually in a pretty precarious place to be: enough serious competitors, for instance, and that's that.

Only world-class companies can withstand an onslaught of competition and disruptive market influences, because only the world-class will have something extra or unique to offer.

What do you need to do to make sure you differentiate yourself from these businesses? How do you avoid the slide into being 'okay'?

As an entrepreneur you need to be taking a larger view of your business, and asking yourself: What particular thing can this group of people, armed with these assets, do which is *world class*?

You might not be able to answer this straight away, but you should keep asking the question until it becomes clear – and by that time you should find that you are already doing it. If not, make those necessary changes: it could entail a reorganisation of some description, increased focus on one or more specific areas, and so on. But identify and adapt, before it is too late.

74.

Know your business's economic engine

You are a business so you depend on profit, and, even more importantly, on profit margin. What single thing would allow you to raise your profit margin – what, in other words, is your business's economic engine?

It might be something pretty simple – and unexpected.

A business networking club that I worked with established, after some research, that the driver of their economic engine was handshakes. The more handshakes made at an event (and the more events they ran), including digital handshakes (or online introductions through websites and social media) then the more business and leads were generated for members. This, of course, increased the perceived value of the networking club for those members and allowed the club to keep earning membership fees, gaining new members and sustaining their prices and profit margins at a high level despite the competition.

The number of handshakes became a measure of the economic engine, and this was the key factor that they measured to see if the business was moving forward, static or at risk of slipping backwards.

75.

Ideas are cheap – unless they are patentable

Protecting your ideas is critical. But you have to protect ideas that are proven in some way. That is, in short, ideas that can be implemented or which customers can be persuaded to buy.

Before you have something substantive to prove it, it remains a cheap and quick idea. Pursue it by all means – but aim to make or break the idea quickly. The faster you can discard the good and the bad ideas, the quicker you can get to the great ideas.

Any entrepreneur worth their salt will throw out new ideas on a weekly if not daily basis.

Don't worry about theft of ideas too early

Don't ask people to sign non-confidentiality forms unless you have already patented your idea. Even then, the chance of someone copying your idea, after briefly talking to you about it, is extremely unlikely. There's no need to be too paranoid.

More importantly, you will be surprised by the number of highly useful and valuable insights that other business people can offer you if you are willing to share your idea and talk about it. Indeed, you may have to tell your idea to 20 or 30 people before you are clear about how best to describe it and how best to communicate it.

I have found it helpful to think of myself as a blacksmith forging an idea. The anvil is provided by other people and my job is to hammer the idea into shape by talking and speaking to other people about it. Without the forging – and the open conversations – you end up with just an ordinary piece of iron.

Young entrepreneurs, in particular, often worry about the theft of their ideas way too early. Yes, if you have run a three-year research project and have devised a unique formula or process you should patent it. However, the ideas around how to market the product or process may be novel, but clearly don't deserve to be wrapped up in the dreaded NDA (non-disclosure agreement).

Share formulae – under a lawyer's guidance

Of course, when you decide to share your key formulae, or the details of how you managed to deliver a change in materials, or anything else particularly cutting edge, exclusive and readily copyable...then you will want people to sign non-disclosure forms.

But this stage is likely to come as part of due diligence when someone is close to investing, or purchasing, from you. Not before! At this point you should have a lawyer on board, advising you when and how to manage the release of such information.

As a rule of thumb, if you don't believe you need to take advice from your lawyer before talking to someone about your idea, then you are unlikely to need to get them to sign a non-disclosure form. If you are unsure if you should be getting advice or not, use the 'would you sue?' test below.

Legalities of protecting ideas

Firstly you should be looking at establishing patents and, of course, making sure that no one else has already registered your patent. For this reason a patent search in somewhere like the British Library is a great place to start, after which you should discuss the results with a patent lawyer. Normally this first conversation will be free.

In addition to patents, you may also wish to protect your brand name. This requires you to register a trademark. The rules on trademarks vary from one legal jurisdiction to another, but there are some key areas, for instance, the EU (European Union), where you can apply for a Europe-wide trademark.

The key for most businesses is to quickly grab the .com domain name for your brand. Possession remains 9/10ths of the law in most developed countries and probably 99% of the law in undeveloped countries. So the smart thing to do is to quickly register your domain name(s). As soon as you own the domain name, and especially if you put a single holding web page on it, then you have begun to assert your claim on that name ahead of anyone else.

So, the simple fact of owning the .com domain name for your brand and using that website will establish a right which is recorded in time. This fact will form the first part of your claim to trademark your brand.

Need more help? Best to get a lawyer involved – just make sure that he or she is a specialist in patents, trademarks and intellectual property; also check out **www.ipo.gov.uk**.

The "Would you sue?" test

Still not convinced that you should be a little more open about discussing your ideas in general terms?

Okay then – before you decide on whether to get the non-disclosure form out of your bag, ask yourself: Would I be willing to sue over this issue? If not, then the paper provides no legal protection.

Still not convinced? Ask your lawyer how easy it would be to sue. Ask what it would cost and the degree of certainty in winning.

The essence of a successful commercial court case is that you need to be able to prove a financial loss. Would you be able to do this? And if you can, will the loss be big enough to cover the cost of your legal fees and make it worth the effort to litigate?

If not, save yourself the trouble, go back to your other 'really good ideas' and make sure you buy the domain name in time.

76.

Live above the shop

Sorry, you can't live on a beach. Yes, as an entrepreneur you do need to live above the shop. That is to say, you need to live near to your business – near enough to not be inconvenienced by spending time in the office, shop, factory or whatever space it is that your business occupies.

When everything is going well, then you don't need to be in the office all the time – but if problems arise, you need to be able to look people in the eye and make decisions about who is telling the truth, who is not telling the truth and who is deluding themselves and you.

Conference calls are great and can bring quick resolution on a number of issues – especially if you have a number of staff out of the office – however, to make the really big decisions you need to 'take the temperature', as it were, and then act on instinct. You can't do this by looking at spreadsheets or quizzing staff on the phone. You simply need to be there. It will involve gut decisions and you want to give yourself the best chance of getting them right.

Spot the rot and stop bad practice

Any carpenter will tell you that, once the rot sets into a piece of wood, it's very hard to save that piece. It's the same with business. Spotting the rot before it takes hold in your business is something you should be aware of and focused on. If you become a little paranoid about this, then you've probably got the emphasis about right. This is why you have to live above the shop.

77.

Remember the risk to your reputation

A key reason for not doing something is reputation risk.

Salespeople, for instance, can get caught by the disease of 'Big Deal-itus'. This is when they are so excited about a huge deal that they fail to see the risks involved and the damage it could do to your business if it distracts key staff and then fails to come in, or worse, if it is agreed but your business is unable to deliver it without harming your reputation with existing customers. You can then either damage your reputation with your new customer, or with the old ones. Great.

Now, this does not mean that you shouldn't take big deals. It just means that you have to consider the cost of the deal going wrong – either before it is signed, or, worse, after it is signed.

If you are big enough or have enough back-up to manage the downside, then you are covered. The mistake is to imagine that this big deal will solve any business problems you have in one swoop. Any such deal rarely does, and if you find yourself thinking "if only we could land the XYZ deal, then we'd be fine" then you are probably about to take a huge reputational gamble.

In some cases, it might make sense to spin out the big deal into a new entity. This will work if you are able to bring new investment into that entity and it is not a subsidiary of your existing business. However, this is a complex and time-consuming process in and of itself, and therefore unlikely to be effective for businesses of less than £2m turnover.

Know how much it will cost if it goes wrong

Entrepreneurs don't always ask, "What will it cost me if it goes wrong?"

This is the simplest measure of whether something is worth worrying about. Obviously, if the cost is a large amount for your business at its current size, then it is a high risk. If the cost is now insignificant to your business, as the business is much bigger, then (within reason) don't worry about it.

Famously, some entrepreneurs have asked, "what will it cost me if I'm caught"? The issue here is that businesses have to step through increasingly high administrative costs, and sometimes it is easier and cheaper to take the risk and pay the fine. Dubious, although sometimes understandable – so long as it doesn't have a major cost for your reputation (see above).

78.

Put it in writing – and make sure *you* sign it

Sorry, no handshake agreements – whether with staff, freelancers, suppliers, customers or competitors. You must have a contract. Okay, a 'heads of agreement', which is halfway to a formal legal contract and states the clear intentions of both parties, or at least a letter – in fact, anything, so long as it is in writing and has a signature and a clear statement of your agreement. (With customers in relatively conventional retail, obviously this will generally just be standard invoices.)

At the end of the day, you are unlikely to enforce a legal contract, but what is written down and signed will allow you to put pressure on the other side to stick to their agreement. Even if you can't enforce the terms of the contract, you will have the upper hand in the moral negotiation, and this counts for more than you might realise.

For instance, if a supplier lets you down and you have to pass on the disappointment to clients, then being able to tell your clients that you have a proper written agreement will reassure them that you are a serious business and worth trusting. If you don't believe me, try telling your clients that you don't bother with written agreements.

Don't worry about the fine legal print

Assuming the key terms are clear, covering...

- what you will do

- what they will do

- what neither of you will do, and

- who and how each party gets paid

...then everything else is of minor importance. Except, perhaps, the ownership of the customer and any intellectual property (if this is applicable).

Worrying too much about the legal small print reduces the likelihood of getting a signed agreement. Remember that an imperfect signed agreement that covers the major points is better than no signed agreement. Therefore, fight on the big points, and give way on the small stuff.

The things 'you won't do'

A contract is designed to protect you and it will protect you if you use it to clearly state what you are going to do, and, more importantly, what you are not going to do.

It is a bad idea to introduce 'won't dos' late into any negotiation, as it could make the other party withdraw in mistrust, confusion or disappointment. If listed out at the beginning of the discussions, you'll find that they will be accepted relatively easily. Don't make the classic mistake of forgetting to list them out in the *first draft* of any contract!

Put the contract in the bottom draw – it won't deliver

At the end of the day, a contract protects the rights of a business, it doesn't make the other party do anything they don't want to do.

Despite the contract, work gets done only when both parties wish to do business and deliver. Therefore, don't rely on the contract to ensure that the other party behaves or delivers.

There are therefore two things to consider.

1. Firstly, if the other party believes the contract to be unfair, then it won't work. The related point here is that there isn't much point in agreeing a broadly unfair contract, as the other party is going to rebel sooner or later.

2. Secondly, you need to make sure that you get what was promised by being vigilant and staying close to the other party – don't think you can take your eyes off the relationship because you have a legal document.

So, once the contract is signed, put it in the bottom draw and leave it there.

Never delegate the contract signing

Yes, with talented managers you can delegate the negotiation of contracts – particularly if they follow the points listed above – however, you should never delegate the signing of contracts.

There are two reasons for this. Firstly, a contract could give away all the rights of your business on a single sheet of paper. You don't want to offer any scope to this risk. Secondly, as per Rule 54, your managers will negotiate more effectively if they (like you) are able to say – "Not sure my chairperson will accept that point – of course, I understand why you want it, but they don't..." and a whole myriad of similar phrases, all of which can be deployed to excellent effect.

Never delegate the cheque signing

Who can pay bills in your business? You!

If it is your business, make sure you pay the bills and sign the cheques. If you really don't want to get involved in the small stuff, then allow a trusted finance director to pay small bills up to £1000 or give credit cards with monthly limits of £1000 to your key managers. But pay all other bills yourself.

This is another reason for turning up in the office on a regular, if not consistent, basis – so you can sign the bills.

Perhaps the most important benefit of this is that the act of paying the bills will help you make sure that you don't let waste grow in the business. If you don't like a cheque that has been presented to you to sign, then query it. Send it back to the manager and ask him or her to prove that it was a good purchase. You may have to pay this bill in the end regardless, but it is a great way to know if your managers are effective at achieving value and it keeps them on their toes.

If you aren't the one signing them off, you may never find out about the bad deals. The moment you pass on the responsibility for paying bills to someone else, you will see weaker cost control and an increase in waste. The only exception to this is if you pass that responsibility to a Rottweiler-like accountant.

Never give personal guarantees

Don't take on personal liabilities for credit cards. Use debit cards instead. Remember, cards have long contracts – one, two or three years – and if your business is new, they'll require a personal guarantee. This is dangerous because you are likely to forget the liability. If you are the 100% shareholder, then the liability in the company is yours wholly, and the responsibility for the debts on those credit cards is more or less the same as a personal liability.

The danger is increased when you have a personal liability but the company is in shared ownership. The other shareholders, who are often also directors, might get the business into trouble or act fraudulently – or even just run off with the money to live on a distant island. If so, any personal guarantees you have provided to banks of the company will be called on and you may find yourself with serious losses – with your partner's liabilities to deal with too.

Business people have lost their homes over personal guarantees that looked innocent at the time but ultimately went wrong.

The best solution is: Don't do personal guarantees.

79.

Understand fixed costs

Most businesses will analyse their costs in terms of fixed costs and variable costs, with the idea that fixed costs can't be easily reduced. Fixed costs tend to be office rent, fully employed staff, and so on – those things you need to pay, even if you have no revenue.

The classic error here is to see any cost as fixed.

The reality is that you can break your rental agreement, you could sublet part of your office and you can let go or reduce the salary of your senior managers. When times are tough, there are *no* fixed costs. There are simply costs for breaking contracts early. You need to know what those costs are on a regular basis, and keep your accountants reporting on them.

Don't worry about balance sheets any more – just ask your accountant for one single, simple number: How much would it cost me to end all contracts? Or put it another way, if we were to close the business today, what would we owe in redundancy, office costs, returned money to customers, etc? You will quickly discover the rapidly growing cost of your long-term employees (should you have any).

There you go – now you know your real fixed costs. And, if you don't like the size of this number, take action to reduce it.

80.

Never let tax drive your decision making

It is a major mistake to create and run a business merely for tax reasons. That is not to say that you cannot save tax – you very often can. It is just the wrong reason to set up and run a business.

Why is this?

Creating and running a business is about pursuing a dream and fulfilling your purpose in life. You will kill the dream if you do it simply for tax reasons. If you let tax be your reason and drive, you are allowing the tail to wag the dog.

Classically, entrepreneurs fail to consider the dullness and energy-sapping nature of dealing with tax schemes and the cost, both in terms of professional time (hiring accountants, lawyers, etc.) and their own time (and what they might better do with it).

Once decided – don't forget to optimise your tax

And, in apparent direct contradiction of the above, you can't forget about tax. That is, once you have decided you are going to create and run a business for far better reasons than tax law, you need to run it in the most efficient way – and that requires you to run it in a tax-efficient way, too.

However, most tax-efficient schemes are expensive to run and complex to administer. Therefore, at an early stage, tax is not likely to be a serious consideration, nor should it preoccupy the entrepreneur.

If you take investment at a later stage, part of the finance might be used to make a change in structure (i.e. moving offshore or setting up a UK EIS – Enterprise Investment Scheme). That is a good use of the money at that point; however, there is little or no point in doing this at the outset, when it is unclear whether your business will ever generate revenue, let alone profit.

81.

Someone has already solved your problem

It is typical to believe that no one else really understands your business problem. And this is usually based on the empirical research of asking your current business colleagues, your current friends/advisors and your wife or husband – and coming up with little in the way of helpful answers.

Well, think about it logically for a moment. If your current group of staff or advisors understood your problem, then it wouldn't be a problem, right? So, logically, problems you have will almost always be problems that your current set of people (yourself included) can't solve or don't know how to begin to solve.

That doesn't mean no one understands your business problem – only that none of your current advisors understand it. You simply have to go searching for someone who has solved a similar problem.

Innovation or advice

Once you accept that your business problems are a function of not yet having found the right advice or solution, then you are faced with the question of whether your problem is genuinely unique.

It is very unlikely to be, but there are times when this is the case. It could be that you are looking to provide a service which simply has no parallel to learn from, and no solutions available off the shelf. Then you must inevitably start the process of resolving the problem by building the tool, machine, business process or business strategy that hasn't yet been built and that will solve it for you.

This method will be very expensive, very time consuming and you'll probably end up with a machine or process that doesn't quite do what it is meant to do and therefore doesn't quite solve the problem. This is a classic but probably unavoidable error. Innovation is messy.

As a side point, you may find that the machine you have built is worth more than the original business idea. Remember boo.com, the fashion retailer? It burnt a lot of cash, went bust but then sold the underlying technology, which many online clothes retail businesses are now built upon.

* * *

The alternative is to say that every business problem I have faced or will face has been solved – at least once – by someone. This is, in 99% of situations, likely to be the case. Maybe 99.9%.

It is just that your business problem hasn't been given to the right person.

This way of seeing the business problem will then lead you on a people search, to find the person who can solve your problem quickly and easily because he or she has already solved that problem somewhere else.

Your people search will be a search for an advisor, a mentor, an agency, a service, a freelancer or a friend: just someone who has solved the problem before. Yes, the time it takes to find someone is unknown; but the more you learn to go searching for someone new, the better you become and the faster you'll solve future as-yet-unknown problems.

Also, when you find the right person or agency, then your problem will be solved quickly and cheaply. This is not fanciful – if the offered solution is expensive and lengthy, it's likely that the person or company offering to solve it hasn't any better ideas than you, and will be quoting accordingly (it will take them time and money to find out themselves).

I recall asking for tax advice on how to manage the tax position between myself and both my Spanish and UK companies. I was quoted €60,000 by one firm who clearly didn't know anything about it, as it would require them to do a lot of research. In the end, I did nothing. I used my existing networks to make the tax issues irrelevant and saved the €60k.

The real cost, then, is your time in building the right network.

Build your professional network

Many entrepreneurs build networks of advisors. I, unfortunately, am not someone who did this naturally. Many other entrepreneurs may fall into my camp, too.

So, if you are like me, you need to make a conscious effort to get out and network. But before you do, let me give you a little bit of focus; namely, you are looking for people who have solved problems. Whilst you might not be aware of any business issues at the moment, by actively searching and building your network with problems in mind, you are creating a web of knowledge and experience that can quickly solve future issues. Moreover, if you are asking other business leaders and advisors about problems they have solved, then you are likely to uncover some issues with your own business that you hadn't considered.

If you are meeting the right people, you should find that new issues and new opportunities come up all the time. If this isn't happening, then you need to change the business people you are mixing with and go and fish for new networks in a bigger pond.

Business networks are strange. They consist of highly connected people but tend to be within fairly narrow groups. That is, the links between groups will be limited – whilst the level of connectivity within the group will be very high.

Therefore, if your current pool of contacts doesn't give you the connection to solve your business problem, start looking for new pools. The solution is rarely to continue extending your networks in your current pool. So, move to a new city, try a different business sector or join the most powerful network group you can find.

Look, this might seem a bit extreme, but Jeff Bezos of Amazon drove from New York to set up his business in Silicon Valley. Why? He needed to tap the talent and skills of San Francisco (he already knew all the money men and deal makers in New York). He was simply expanding his network to find people who had already solved his new business problems.

82.

Put business before technology

The error of rushing to build technology solutions before any merited business purpose is identified was typified by the rush to build dot-com businesses during the dot-com boom. "Build it and they will come," was the war cry. Many, many businesses were built, generally based on technology rather than sound business; a few drew some customers, and only a very few kept any customers.

No one will repeat this mistake with technology now, will they? Oh yes they will!

This error is repeated in businesses everyday. If you have a technical team then you will be tempted to find projects to keep them employed. The loss may not be as disastrous as basing your whole company around a speculative innovation, but it will build up and eat away at your efficiency.

So, how do you stop this happening? Simple. Firstly, use freelancers. Secondly, if you receive plans for a technology project, turn it down unless it is clear how it will benefit your customers and your business. There is nothing to say that the plan cannot be worked on and improved so that it does benefit them, but till it does, reject it.

The point is that there must be a clear and established business *need* – not an intuitive guess or instinct – before any such build project begins.

Avoid big bang technology developments

Many businesses lose their way on technology developments because they are attempting to build a great solution all at once. Something that promises to 'revolutionise' an aspect of your business is a typical example of a mistaken project.

Here's what normally happens with this classic error:

- The tech guys are so excited about the development that resources are drawn off day-to-day work and focused on this big improvement.

- Then the deadline slips; another big push is required. Less day-to-day work is accomplished.

- Then the deadline slips again; a few issues start to be raised. No day-to-day work is accomplished.

- More issues are raised. But now the successful system has become so important that you let the deadline slip again.

- You may now demand that the system is just put live. If you do, you'll probably find that it doesn't do what was hoped for – the size of the project was too big or too ambitious for the team or the resources that your company was able to offer.

- The project will be quietly mothballed.

Instead, projects, even if you are a major IT developer, should be released on the basis of little and often. Most high quality technical developers can create and release a prototype within a week that will deliver 80% of the functionality in a raw format.

If this is not possible, then the project is almost bound to fail. Therefore, hold your developers to this method. And, if they can release a prototype within a week, then every week they can make substantial improvements to that prototype for your agreement and sign off.

If not, then the project is unlikely to ever see the light of day and should be avoided.

Release all technical developments on Monday at 9 am

Don't choose a Thursday or Friday to release technical or software developments, as your technical team will always need slightly longer and then late on Friday your technical staff will tell you that it is better not to release new updates just before the weekend, in case the systems run into problems when no one is in the office.

The solution is to always schedule your release for Monday at 9 am and ensure that your technical developers don't leave the office on Friday until the Monday release is ready to go. So, set your review meeting up for 9 am on Monday morning. This means that if the tech guys need to work over the weekend, then they will.

This all sounds rather brutal, I know, and my point isn't that you need to be a monster, or even that the tech guys really will end up working weekends. It's that this framework will help concentrate their minds and encourage them to only back viable projects in the first place, and to work on them as efficiently as possible when they're green lighted.

Using this timing and method will be a test of both their ongoing commitment to the project and their ability to deliver it. And, never forget – all such projects are speculative and you may have to end the project at any stage.

83.

Control credit

Good credit control is necessary, but even better is to establish a payment plan that requires up-front payment.

However, credit control starts with your customer contracts. If you have established the right to ask for payment within 15 days and the right to withdraw the service if the bill is unpaid, then you are in a strong position and it is easy to implement.

If you have no contract, then you can have no credit control.

Too many entrepreneurs make the mistake of not getting their contracts in order until it is too late.

Control unlimited liabilities

Mobile phones and expense accounts are typically an uncontrolled liability and could get your business into difficulty if managed poorly.

You can cap credit cards and require that they are used for signed-off purchases (not travel) and that all travel expenses are claimed back personally. The chore of claiming travel expenses encourages staff not to spend the money in the first place.

84.

Tough decisions are the right ones

Entrepreneurs and business leaders constantly have to make decisions. Some are easy, but others are tough.

A tough business decision is usually difficult mostly in an emotional sense. It requires you to disappoint someone or upset someone, perhaps quite badly. It might require you to go back on a promise you made previously. However, I have found that if I am balancing two decisions that seem roughly equal and one is easy and the other tough, then nearly always it is the tough decision that is the correct one. This is because we are emotionally hardwired not to take tough decisions and tend to be biased towards the easy ones. *If a hard and an easy decision lie in the balance, it is likely that the easy one does so somewhat on the basis of this bias, and is therefore not equally good at all.*

Making emotionally tough decisions is a critical part of growing as a leader but also of convincing those around you that you are worth following. If your team sees that you don't have the capacity for tough decisions, they will not have much trust in your leadership – even if it means letting some of their colleagues go, or something else unpleasant but necessary.

It does take a leader to ignore the short-term upset and bad feeling and stick with the longer-term plan to create a sustainable business. However, be open about tough decisions to both those affected directly and indirectly. It creates a sense of trust and confidence in your leadership whilst also helping those who are affected by the decision to let go and move to be successful in some other way.

85.

Plan your exit from your business

Selling your business for £10m sounds like a great achievement. However, if you are the CEO/entrepreneur then the buyer will want to tie you in. So, sticking with the £10m example, typically a buyer would offer a £5m cash payment and then a further £5m in two years' time, subject to the business achieving certain revenue or profit goals after sale, perhaps a doubling of revenue over the two year period.

And don't forget, if you as the entrepreneur have given away equity in the business (a perfectly normal situation to be in) and now only have, say, a 20% stake, you can expect no more than £1m now and £1m in two years. Suddenly the headline figure is no longer so remarkable.

And you pay tax in both cases, of course.

Now we've gone from a feeling of being on the brink of incredible riches to being able to buy a nice terraced house in London. It's great, but it's not quite the same.

Here is another approach: Build and sell your first business for whatever you can, on the basis that you are not involved in the business post-sale. Simple. Don't pay any attention to workout fees. Get the best value you can, by making sure your business really is sustainable and can operate without you and demonstrating this to the buyers. However, whatever you do, once you've decided to sell don't hang around. Take the money, buy the new house and start another business or three.

Don't get tied in when the business is sold

Why isn't it a good idea to just stick it out and put the two years (or whatever agreed figure) in and recoup the full fee in due course? The problem is that entrepreneurs often lose interest once the control has passed on and they no longer have the same kind of freedoms or sense of control as before. They fall short of the goals that they were willing to set at the point of sale, and therefore fail to collect the other half (£5m in this example) of the sale contract. They just waste two years.

There is, of course, an alternative. And that is, if you want to bank £10m, then create a business that would sell for £20m, such that when the owners offer you half up-front – £10m – you simply accept it and walk away. Don't negotiate for the remaining £10m bonus by agreeing to work to achieve the new owner's business targets.

The insolvency exit

The other business exit is insolvency or closing the business down. Typically this comes about because you run out of cash, or you realise the business can't make money and therefore cannot sell itself for more than the value of its assets.

You need to plan for this (hopefully remote) contingency – which means you need to have enough cash to live on for six months, preferably 12, if things go wrong. I don't mean money invested in property or even shares or bonds. I mean bank deposits. Yes, interest-earning bank deposits, but bank deposits all the same.

If you have this cash available, and so long as you don't make yourself personally liable for any business debt, then you will have the financial strength to allow yourself to recover.

And recovery is the most important thing, because it allows you to start again. This time, like me, you will be carrying a few scars but armed with deep experience. If you are still in reasonable financial shape and healthy, then you will be in a much stronger position to start again.

Exit according to the business cycle

The biggest mistake an entrepreneur can make is not selling their business when the market for selling businesses is strong. Again, I made the classic mistake of letting the shareholders' business goal of reaching a fixed financial valuation target (of £20m) get in the way of this decision.

The business cycle will have periods of strong business sales and then periods when nothing sells unless very heavily discounted. It is far better to sell at the top of the business cycle, when revenue sales are strong but profit margins are beginning to come under pressure, even if you don't achieve the original sale goal that you had in mind, than it is to hang on.

Why? Business cycles are typically from five to seven years in duration. The US National Bureau of Economic Research found 32 business cycles over the period 1854 to 2001. Hence, if you miss the top of this business cycle you will need to wait another five to seven years before you can sell for the best price again. Do you really want to wait up to seven years? (Assuming, too, that your business survives the inevitable downturn.)

Don't forget, entrepreneurs need the excitement of the new. Will you cope with up to seven years' hard grind for little or no reward? Honest answers, please.

Consider all offers

If you get an offer to sell, consider it carefully and don't dismiss it right away. Even if it is a low offer, it gives you the excuse to go to the market and see what someone else might pay. If this enquiry is driven by the fact that you have already had an offer, then you look neither desperate nor hungry. It can be a great way to smoke out other players and then let them bid the price up.

Equally, when it comes to the point of concluding a sale, don't let the opportunity slip for a few per cent discount. The buyer is going to try all sorts of tactics to get the price down and whilst you can battle your way through this, be prepared to give some ground.

It is like that old saying 'a bird in the hand is worth two in the bush' – cash in the hand is worth twice what someone else *might* have paid for it.

And remember, your entrepreneurial career doesn't stop here – it just takes a new and more exciting path!

Some birds migrate

As an entrepreneur, sometimes it is just time to move on. It is not about the money, it is often more about your gifts and what you think of as your purpose in life. If what you are doing does not fit you anymore, then sell it and move on.

As an entrepreneur you will have a natural love of the new. Sometimes, you may find that you have been doing the same old thing for too long and it is simply time to move on.

In which case, accept your fate, and do just that – move on.

Some birds migrate every season to find new feeding grounds. Entrepreneurs are similar. If it is time to go, go quickly and with the minimum of fuss. Don't wait for the last penny or worry whether the business met the original business and financial goals. If you can leave with a profit, then it is time to go.

There are new feeding grounds that await you. Even a modest profit will set you up well for the next venture, and, most importantly, you will be surprised by who will follow you.

86.

Avoid management and board meetings

In some cases the entrepreneur will give up running the business and shift to controlling their shares and share value via a board of directors or a CEO. In this case, you would wish the CEO to propose the brand strategy and pricing strategy (and therefore profit margin strategy), but this should always be under the final say-so of the shareholders.

However, until shareholders have someone else to hold accountable (i.e. the entrepreneur has sold a big chunk of his or their shares), then board meetings are useless and to be avoided, with the exception of allowing an entrepreneur to engage non-executive directors at his or her board meeting.

Management meetings are similar. If you have an accountant, then your accountant should be providing you with the data and key business measures talked about in these Rules. If you are not getting this information, get a new accountant – but don't start management meetings until you want to hold your managers accountable for profit margin.

Non-exec rule for allowing board meetings

A board meeting is where the non-executive directors (i.e. those people who have a director-level responsibility to the business but don't run the business on a day-to-day basis) hold the CEO and their executive directors responsible for the results.

The non-executive directors will always have the interest of the shareholders in mind and may conflict with the CEO and executives on issues such as capital investments, dividends and executive pay. These conflicts are healthy and should be encouraged. They will help to ensure that suitable checks and balances are placed on the paid CEO and their team.

However, the cost and effort of such a structure is significant and therefore only sensible for businesses turning over more than £1-£5m, or where a third party (i.e. not an executive director) has made a substantial cash investment.

If none of these apply, then keep your meeting to management meetings and avoid the formalised board structure.

Of course, if you wish to raise a large amount of cash, then potential investors will want to see a strong non-exec team, as it will reassure them that their money is safe. This additional non-exec oversight and control is one of the hidden costs of raising funds.

Ensure spreadsheets are circulated prior to important meetings

All board or management meetings or reviews of business performance will require spreadsheets of some kind.

To enable everyone to engage in the assumptions behind the spreadsheets, the documents need to be distributed 24 hours before the meetings. This allows people at the meeting to familiarise themselves with the spreadsheets and then be ready to ask questions about the assumptions behind the calculations.

If it is not possible to distribute the spreadsheets before the meeting, then cancel the meeting instead. And ask the person responsible for the delay to rearrange the meeting. Require all attendees to raise questions about the spreadsheet so that they are fully engaged.

Managers must be prepared

Poorly presented proposals or spreadsheets that are not circulated prior to key management meetings are often met with the reply, "Sorry, I'll do better next time." Should you give them another chance?

Yes, if they can identify what they will do differently next time.

No, if they fail repeatedly. Twice is to repeat an error. Three times is to make it permanent.

Spreadsheets reveal assumptions – so discuss the assumptions

New enterprises need to establish a monthly review mechanism, even if it is just a quick sit around the table to review the bank statements. These meetings will often focus on future plans (or earnings) that will be expressed in spreadsheets.

However, as the business grows, the spreadsheets may become dangerously complex as they attempt to express a greater number of variables.

The result is that directors and non-exec directors may travel many miles and expend much effort to meet together to sit and read through spreadsheets desperately trying to understand how they were constructed and the true meaning behind them.

This is fatal. The real value of a senior management discussion is that it questions the underlying assumptions about the business plan and/or business model.

This process of questioning will highlight whether you have potential price issues, cash-flow issues or capital issues. The degree to which these become serious problems depends on whether you believe the sales forecasts and assumptions behind the plan. So engage with the assumptions early to avoid the classic mistake of being taken by surprise.

Once you have your spreadsheets arriving in good time, the next step is to ensure that the meeting focuses on the assumptions behind the spreadsheet, not the spreadsheets themselves. A discussion on why revenue will grow in a given geography or product division or why a new product will achieve additional sales is a far better use of time than a discussion about whether the numbers in the spreadsheet add up.

A meeting which spends its early energy on deciphering spreadsheets will fail to make any headway against the key issues.

Avoid the 'sudden increase in profit in year three (or five)' business forecast error

This classic mistake shows only that it is hard to justify cost increases three years into a business plan, not that those cost increases won't happen. Typically a successful business will draw competitors, or a too successful business may draw governmental changes that require an increase in marketing or an increase in production costs.

Any business which has a profit margin of 30% or more is going to be a highly attractive target for other expanding businesses and, therefore, unless there is a compelling reason why 'no one can imitate' or 'no government dare ban or legislate', then it is dangerous to assume ever-increasing profit margins.

No questions? Don't come!

The key to successful meetings is to keep them small.

Anyone at the meeting who is not raising questions about the spreadsheets' assumptions and therefore underlying issues behind the business performance won't need to attend future management meetings.

Simple. (And they'll thank you for it.)

This is a great way to keep your key meetings small and help maintain the focus. You can always invite people to attend the meeting as a guest, but you should only keep those people who are willing and able to dig into the depths of the business plan to be a part of the meeting.

Discussing potential ideas

You may wish to spend some time discussing half-developed ideas. This should be less about whether the idea is going to work and more about whether you wish to spend time and resources working out if the idea is a good one.

In other words, the purpose of the meeting is not to do the work of proving the idea, it is to decide if the idea fits your business and deserves resourcing to establish a credible plan – which can be discussed at next month's meeting.

87.

Use the envelope test

If you find that you or your team can't deliver simple and clear spreadsheets, even when devising or presenting your business plan, do this: Write a summary of your business plan on the back of an envelope.

If it won't fit, then it won't work, because it is too complex.

Business plans have to be the kind of thing that everyone in your business, at every level, can grasp and act out in their corner of the enterprise every day. They have to be the kind of thing that outside investors, too, can grasp quickly. And good business ideas rarely come at the end of an epic sequence of propositions, qualifications and statistics. They should be explicable simply and directly. So break out the envelopes and start writing.

Equally, if your team is in love with spreadsheets, then throw the notebooks and projectors out of the room and ask them to write their presentations on a whiteboard instead. If they can't write proposals, reviews or anything else on a whiteboard or even an envelope or just a napkin, then throw them out with their idea. He or she can always come back when they have got clear about their proposal.

88.

Marketing comes first, design second

Too often the design of the marketing pack becomes overly fixated upon, and the most important part of marketing. It is not. It is the list of customers (potential or actual) to which you send the marketing pack which really counts.

Just as it's the traffic to your website that matters more than the website itself, once you've surpassed the basic hurdle of having something competent and professional-looking up there. If you have great traffic to your one-page website with a clear phone number displayed for potential clients to contact you, you will generate more enquiries than a superb or flashy looking website with no traffic.

So this marketing mistake is easy to avoid – simply don't let the design drive the marketing decisions. The point is that design is an activity that FOLLOWS everything else – it does not lead it. It is a classic mistake to start designing something before you know who it is for, or how you are going to get your design in front of your prospective clients or customers.

Don't forget design

The related or opposite error is, of course, to pay no attention to design whatsoever.

Design's role in marketing is to make your brand and offer clearly distinguishable from all the other brands and offers in your marketplace. Hence absence of design will just make your brand and offer look comparatively careless and shabby when placed next to competitors. Or it means it just won't be noticed at all.

Don't fall for the trap of developing flashy design just to be different in the way that some teenagers choose to dress in an attempt to shock and be noticed. Instead, look at the accuracy and clarity with which the design conveys your brand and offer.

Measure design not by whether you think it is pretty or nice, but by whether or not it sharpens your message and distinguishes you from your competition.

Avoid the 'got money – so let's spend' mistake

Many marketing campaigns start to go wrong when money is spent – or perhaps just made available for spending.

Marketing is possible without spending money; and unless you have substantial marketing experience, you are likely to spend that money badly. Most marketing objectives can be achieved by hard work. So, for instance, instead of buying lists of names, spend time building your own list. It is likely to be slower and harder work, but won't be out of date.

However, pressure is often placed on marketing teams to deliver more leads yesterday! This is where the quest for bigger marketing budgets begins and where you may well see a fall off in return of leads or sales for your marketing budget.

Measure, measure, measure

With so many opportunities to spend your marketing budget, it will be hard to know which marketing methods to choose. Often marketing novices will simply spread the cash around a bit and see what happens.

This is okay if you:

- never spend more than 10% of your total budget on any single activity or in any single month

- set clear measurable goals and outcomes

- measure the success of each marketing spend against those goals.

If you spend only 10% of your budget finding out what works and doesn't work, then you have 90% remaining to focus on the most effective marketing method or methods. Typically, new entrepreneurs will do the reverse and spend 90% of their marketing budget on something that doesn't work, and get neither tangible results nor any idea of why it didn't work.

They then want someone else to deliver their remaining marketing objectives based on the 10% of the budget left. This is not going to work.

Avoid falling for the next big marketing thing

Marketing tends to generate a lot of hype around new techniques.

Hence, when something new comes along, like social media, everyone gets excited about it because they think everyone else is getting excited about it, and soon everyone starts doing it because they think everyone else is doing it. Presently, everyone *is* doing it. This is called the snowball effect.

When you see or experience a snowball effect, the first thing to do is to jump out of the way. Then decide if you want to join in – and why – or, alternatively, go in the exact opposite direction.

In essence, if everyone is spending money on, say, sending email marketing, then you will do far better if you put your marketing in the post instead. Why? Because no one else is doing it and therefore there is little or no competition for your marketing message to be seen or heard.

In time, the hype around the next big thing will die down and then it will take its proper place in the marketing mix – just as search engine ranking (all the rage two years ago) is now seen as old hat, but search engine optimisation (SEO), where websites are carefully constructed so as to enable customers to find them through key words on Google and so forth, has become one of several key components in successful promotion.

Meanwhile, be willing to go against the tide. You'll often find you can get further.

89.

Set in place a feedback loop

Whereas businesses used to advertise in local or trade press, now they spend their advertising money on their own websites and social media, iPhone content, videos and digital media.

This new digital marketing environment allows them to quickly and constantly find out what their customers like and don't like, both through more readily running small marketing and communications campaigns, and from being able to access a whole range of statistics on how people respond – whether links were clicked, videos watched, websites read (and for how long), comments left; where, when, who these people were exactly; and so on.

Previously, with traditional advertising, you never knew how your customer responded to your adverts without very expensive customer sampling. Now you can see it all at the click of a mouse.

And this allows you to set in place a key feedback loop (a fancy buzz phrase for 'virtuous circle'). In short, keep feeding the information of customers, and their responses to your marketing, back to the development of your products and services, and you'll soon find that you end up with better and better marketing – and better and better products.

Let me give you an example. I run a digital publication. We launched (and thereby tested) a new page for this publication – Jobs – and found that this became the most popular page on our site almost straightaway. What did that tell us? Our readers were strongly interested in potential jobs. Hence, we gave this page a greater prominence in our digital magazine, spent more editorial time writing about jobs and potential jobs and focused our ad sales team on selling job adverts. So, our publication was improved by a greater understanding of how people were responding to and using it on a day-to-day basis – something that would not have been at all easy in the days of print.

90.

Solve problems with three-way conversations

Don't let problems fester or gather speed. Instead, find a way to dispel them quickly and efficiently.

One of the most effective ways of dealing with 99% of problem situations is the three-way conversation. It works in the flesh and by phone call.

Let's say John has a concern about the design of your new marketing pack, which is being managed by Jack. John phones you up and starts to talk (indirectly, usually) about his worries. When you realise what his real concerns are, you stop him briefly and say, "Let's get Jack in on this conversation."

What then happens?

- Firstly, John learns that gossip isn't any good, and is likely to take the view that in future he'll only raise issues if he is willing to stand by or express his concerns or worries – it is no good muttering at the back of the class.

- Secondly, Jack might be about to make a serious mistake. Jack will probably have an explanation for what he is doing and raise objections to John's concerns.

- Thirdly, either Jack will realise his mistake or John will realise that he hadn't fully considered the issues; or you might not have an agreement (but this is actually very rare).

If you really cannot have agreement, then you potentially have to make a decision and go for it, or you need to pull the parties together for a bigger investigation. Either way, you can quickly get to the bottom of the issue, resolve it if that is possible, or bring forward a special meeting or extra research before going ahead with the plan.

The other benefit of three-way conversations is that people learn to get in touch with you when they have genuine concerns – they know you'll deal with it and not fob them off. In addition, they know that you'll expect them to be able to articulate those concerns confidently, in detail, and in front of others.

This is an excellent way to stop gossiping and back-biting, too, as it puts the issues out in the open.

91.

Avoid shareholders

Any rules about shareholders could fill a book, with the only disadvantage that it would be exceptionally dull. Managing shareholders is about as far from the excitement of being an entrepreneur as you can imagine. Don't do it unless you really, really have to.

If you really do need shareholders, accept in advance the worst-case scenario that you will one day be ousted (see section 'Avoid the horror of the shareholder collective' – Rule 92) and a professional manager put in your place. If this happens, you cannot and should not bother trying to fight it: Take the money and run – you will have been lucky to escape.

The greater the number of shareholders, the greater the opportunity for disagreement. And, if there is no single controlling shareholder, forcing agreement will be difficult.

You are in business (I hope) for the fun and excitement of creating something new, of creating something from nothing. Be careful that your hunger for finance doesn't lead you to sell out on your dream before you even get started.

Or make sure you get tag-along rights

Okay, if you do need to accept other shareholders – and it may be necessary – then ensure that if one shareholder arranges for a sale of their shares, you can sell your shares to the same buyer for the same price too.

This prevents one shareholder selling early to the detriment of the others. It is called tag-along rights.

The way this should work is as follows:

> Shareholder John has 20% of the shares, and establishes an offer for all his shares at £10 each.

> All the remaining shareholders can also elect to sell 20% of their shares to the same buyer at the same price.

> Therefore, if all other shareholders elect to sell, John is only able to sell his part (i.e. one fifth of the total) to this buyer.

> This would mean that John is able to sell 4% of all shares (i.e. 20% of his holding) and remains a shareholder with 16%.

This mechanism ensures that John can't cut and run and that all shareholders are treated equally. It also means that if John really wants to exit, he is more likely to find a buyer for the whole business and therefore create an exit for all shareholders.

92.

Never let family be shareholders

It has been said that family are good fellow shareholders. Why? Because, families are supposed to be able to work together and sort these things out – they can't, after all, escape from each other.

But that is precisely the problem.

Family members, brothers and sisters, brothers-in-law, parents and so on, can't disagree politely and go their different ways. Therefore, they are forced to a consensus. Often the consensus is the weakest option and at least one member of the family will be disappointed; sometimes severely disappointed.

Similarly, poor dividend returns on the family-owned shares will require an overhaul of the direction and management of the business. This is only possible if two things are in place:

1. there is a concentration of shares in the hands of one family member

2. the management and shareholders are not the same.

The worst-case scenario is when family members are also the managers, who are also earning salaries and having to set each other's rates of pay. This scenario is ripe for disaster. Successful family businesses are only successful when the shares are concentrated in the hands of one person, or the management and shareholdings are clearly kept apart.

Just to give you a picture of the worst of all worlds, imagine a collective shareholder structure (that is where no one shareholder has control and big decisions need to be agreed among a number of shareholders), with a large holding held by family members who are also key managers or directors in the business. You need an extremely cooperative and close team to make this structure work because it requires a very high level of agreement in many decisions, and even then it is liable to sudden and repeated collapses in agreement. Plus family members are unlikely to be able to disagree politely.

My first business ended up in this structure and I had good friends and close family working with me. As a group we were often of a common mind and willing to compromise and find agreement. Nevertheless, despite the quality of the people, the structure destined us to regular bouts of political fighting and disagreements.

Don't do it – and don't allow it to happen by slowly giving away parts of the shares to friends, family or fellow directors.

Get professional shareholders

Professional shareholders are better because you don't have to wake up next to them or share your Christmas turkey with them.

They might not be nice to you, but they are more likely to keep you from doing something to damage the business; they have an impartial and outsider's interest in preserving the value of their shares, which means preserving the value of yours too!

In fact, you want shareholders who can tactfully and pleasantly tell you what they think you need to do and make sure you do it. So, find shareholders who can be honest in a pleasant way. If you have to swallow hard medicine, it helps if it is (occasionally) sugar coated.

Avoid quick buck shareholders

Be aware that many shareholders are simply looking to cash in once the business has reached certain milestones. This might be too early for you and stop you getting what you wanted to achieve. But, so long as the sale price is good enough, cash in.

Remember, you can lose your shares, you can lose your business (through bankruptcy), but you can never lose the ability to start new businesses.

Avoid the horror of the shareholder collective

Warren Buffett, the world's most fêted investor, won't invest in a company unless someone has clear control (or will have, following his investment). Of course, he prefers that someone who will hold 51% of shares to be him (or his company) but that is partly for tax reasons.

The point is that he believes a collective shareholder structure – where no one person or group has control – to be a deeply inefficient structure. And he is right! Ignore Mr Buffett at your peril.

If you opt for a collective shareholder structure then you will:

- need regular board meetings which act as oversight on your work

- spend a lot of your time in managing expectations before and after the board meetings

- accept that if your key managers are also shareholders, then they will also spend a lot of time managing expectations and building support for their favoured projects

- as a group, spend less time running the business and will have to delegate more work faster than you might otherwise have done

- accept that what made you an entrepreneur or a director (i.e. you were great at running sales teams, let's say) doesn't make you a great political deal broker in a collective shareholder structure, and, therefore, you and your fellow directors may be poor at managing this structure.

All in all, you have another classic mistake in the making – a deeply inefficient structure which draws away the skill and energy of the founder and his or her partners and leaves a sense of division, which will run through the whole business.

No wonder Mr Buffett doesn't want anything to do with it – and neither should you!

93.

Debt is like a disease

Debt destroys your flexibility and slowly eats away at your enterprise. It forces you to crystallise your business plan early on – which is a sensible idea – but then doesn't allow you to adapt that business plan to reality.

In the years that you implement your plan, your market will change; your competitors will adapt and improve; and so on. Unfortunately, your debt position won't change – and it will therefore be much harder to change your business plan. You'll need the agreement of the creditors, which whilst not impossible, can certainly prove difficult.

The key question here is this: Are you absolutely sure that your idea will work, can be implemented profitably and won't change?

If so, then debt is manageable. If you think, not that you won't succeed, but that your plans may change or your focus may shift when you discover the true costs of operating in your ultimate niche, and you want to retain the freedom to innovate, then debt is likely to hold you back and restrict you.

Of course, there is also the cost of servicing that debt; simply making these regular interest payments will require plenty of time and effort.

The 'debt focuses the mind' fallacy

Some people advise that taking on debt helps to focus the mind and deliver a better result. This may be true when a business has become lazy or complacent. However, is it true when you are starting out? You are already risking your reputation and the fact that you might not earn a decent wage (or any wage) for six, 12 or 18 months.

Isn't that enough of an incentive? Usually it is. My experience is that truly entrepreneurial people don't need debt to be motivated.

Of course, if your business is now successful and you can relax and mess about with it, then yes, someone investing in the business may wish you to take on lots of debt – simply to push you out of the comfort zone and get you motivated again. And that makes some sense.

However, in the first instance, debt is usually a killer for a new business.

When you must take debt – take lots

Many new businesses need three rounds of funding, if they need one. It's simply to do with the difficulty of predicting and forecasting business costs, environment and market response to the new product, and the fact that everything takes longer than it should.

Ask any experienced business angel and they will tell you that this requirement for three rounds of funding happens again and again.

So, if you are going to take debt and think you need £200k, ask for £600k – on the basis that you will always need two further rounds of funding.

Offer to place the additional two rounds' worth of funding (£400k) to one side (in escrow) and not touch it without either the agreement of the creditors or the achievement of pre-set milestones – but make sure that the money is committed at the outset.

Business angels will take the view that you know what you are talking about – rather than think you are being greedy.

Why a little debt is worse than none

If you don't get the three rounds of funding upfront, then the chances are that the little bit of debt you do raise will kill you.

Not only will your funds raised be small, but the cost of raising them will be a very large percentage of what you receive. Therefore, your principal business activity and cost will become raising funds.

This will prevent you from focusing on how to build your business and puts the entire enterprise at risk. Therefore avoid small amounts of debt at all costs, unless you can't, in which case, fill your boots (and get ready to accept the consequences of shareholders and non-exec board meetings).

94.

Build a strong non-exec team – prudently

The good news about funding is that it will help you build your non-exec team. The lenders will want their man or woman on the board and that will drive the creation of a properly constructed non-exec team.

A non-exec director is someone who does not have day-to-day control of the business but is responsible for holding the managing director and his or her executive team to account. They will be part time, well paid and should come with bucketloads of experience and fat contact books.

The non-exec team is there to ensure the investors' money is well spent and that business value is maximised.

And, if they decide that you have reached the end of your contribution as the manager and leader of the business, they'll vote you out of the business. So build your non-exec team knowing that they can throw you off the board.

95.

Understand the three stages of a business

Any new business will go through three stages:

1. pre-revenue

2. pre-profit

3. re-launch or expansion.

It is also highly probable that these will be three stages of fundraising. It takes longer than expected to achieve the initial revenue, longer than expected to turn a profit and it is harder to re-launch or expand than first imagined.

So be careful when giving away equity (shares in your business) to those investing in the pre-revenue phase. At this first stage, the shares appear valueless (a share of nothing!) and investors will ask for a large chunk. But, as an entrepreneur, if you give away 40% of your share of the business at each stage, you will end up after three rounds with just 22%.

Here's how the maths works:

You start with 100%.

- In the first round, you give away 40% and end up with 60% remaining.

- In the second round, you give away 40% of your 60% and are left with 36%.

- In the third round, you give away 40% of your 36% and your share is now just 21.6%.

Are you okay with figures like that? The fact is you may well have to give up a share at some stage, so the best thing is to try to get past at least one or two stages without doing so. If you were able, in the above example, to take your business past the pre-revenue stage – in other words, making sales before asking for money – then with only two rounds of funding left, and 40% departing at each stage, you would end up with 36% of your original holding, rather than 21%. That is 70% more – and means you can sell out and achieve your exit goal earlier.

The difference is, of course, significant. For a business selling for £20m and netting £10m in the up-front payment, it is the difference between a £3.6m pay out and a £2.1m payout. One amount will set you up for life, the other will buy you a house, pay your taxes but won't provide a pension to go along with it.

Investors know that the outcome of the entrepreneur giving away so much is huge, so they are, in fact, naturally suspicious of pre-revenue investment opportunities – they suggest that the entrepreneur lacks experience and, therefore, is probably not the greatest bet.

If your idea is good, get it to the stage of some revenue before you seek funds. And whether and if you seek investment at this stage really comes down to this: Will it damage the long-term value of the business and its assets or intellectual property, if you *delay* raising funds?

If you can make a clear case of why delay will damage the value of the business – or, more particularly, the value of the intellectual property – then you have a strong case for very early investment. If not, either get your business proposal to the point where this argument is clearly made, or better still, get it earning money.

Avoid speculating business angels

Entrepreneurs can make the classic mistake of believing that all business angels and sources of finance are the same. And that once they get sight of cash, then they must have it at any cost.

They get so excited about the smell of money that they forget to ask if it is the right *kind* of money. Is the business angel truly an angel, or the kiss of death for your business? Sometimes, they'll be one and sometimes they really will be the other. So what should you look to avoid?

The worst kinds of business angels are those who:

* require no accountability

* are seeking to trade your business value.

By 'trading your business value', I mean that these business angels are looking only to take advantage of buying at a low price and selling at a high one. Nothing else is of much interest. They will require or request a low price to begin with, and then drive the business to achieve inflated goals that make for a great sales story – and then sell their shares, after which your business may see a drop in sales, or an increase in customer dissatisfaction or some other consequence of driving the revenue forward too quickly.

This is why tag-along rights are so important (see Rule 91). Business angels, of course, want to make money out of an investment, and much of that can be through buying in low and selling out high, but that should not be the only reason they're interested. There isn't much angelic about speculation – you want someone committed to helping and allowing you to grow a sustainable, long-term profitable business.

96.

No share options

Share options, which are rights to buy shares in the future at a discount price, usually have a horrible fixed nature. Essentially, you give out share options based on what you think each individual team member will do. More often than not, however, some employees deliver greater results than others. Some will disappoint terribly, yet still be in possession of the options.

There is a solution. Make all options expire with immediate effect on the person leaving the business (even if they are leaving because they were dismissed or their contract was cancelled). This effectively allows you to take back the options at any time.

However, there is an even better approach that more and more entrepreneurs are beginning to recognise, and that is to give out options once they have been *earned*. Put simply, you hold back from granting options until you are close to a business sale. At this point, you then award them to your key managers for what they have done and also for what commitments they are willing to make to the new owner.

This allows you to have soft conversations early in the life of the business to discuss what 'might be possible', without ever having to commit (at all times making sure that everyone understands that this is a goodwill gesture based on ongoing commitment).

The weakness of the flexible option is that you can't offer this option to everyone in the business, but perhaps that is not such a bad thing. Options are difficult things to value and all but your most senior managers will be suspicious of them, or, worse still, afford them no value.

Remember that at the point of sale of your business to new owners, the acquiring business will be looking to secure the commitment of your talented team. This is the point where your team can start to negotiate better rates and terms. It is a bit like a football team being promoted to the Premiership – they all expect a pay rise on winning the crucial game, but cannot get paid high rates until the team actually *arrives* in the top flight.

For this reason, whilst you may choose to offer share options to certain key members close to the sale, this is more a way of saying 'thanks'. It's got to be a gesture rather than a giveaway, I'm afraid: you don't want the value to become so large that they demotivate that person from working for the new owners, as the business valuation will partly depend on the goodwill of your team transferring to the acquiring business.

Use employee shares if you have a share market

If you want to share the business with all employees, then give them shares, sold or given at the full price/value. However, this only makes sense if you have a business large enough to handle an informal mechanism that allows them to price and sell their shares. Therefore these are best avoided for new enterprises.

However, if you are taking over a large turn-around business, this might be a way of gaining goodwill and sharing in any upturn after a number of very tough years.

97.

Let yourself be ousted – at the right price

One of the biggest fears of entrepreneurs is that outside shareholders will oust them. This nearly happened to me once, and I resisted like crazy. Bad move! It would have been far better to let them oust me by buying my shares and then for me to go and do something new.

For a first business, this is going to be a huge emotional wrench, but by the time you are on the second business, it will be easy.

Just make sure your contract sets out the terms under which you can be ousted and that this includes the purchase of your shares at a pre-agreed rate based on revenue (not profit – you might not have reached that stage).

Good, you've accepted that you can be ousted. Now you need to focus on your personal terms with the company and your exit agreement. As an entrepreneur you will almost certainly never write yourself a proper contract of employment or protect yourself. Why should you, it's your business, right? Only, it isn't…

As soon as you take on debt or receive investment, it is no longer your business. You need to accept that fact quickly and get over it. Equally, as soon as you owe someone some money (a creditor), they have rights over your business too.

Therefore, before you take on any debt or receive the investment you need, make sure that you have a properly constructed contract that rewards you if you are thrown off the board and protects your shareholder value. Typically, if you are ejected you will want to sell all or some of your shares. Make sure your contract allows you to do this at a minimum price per share.

The minimum share price can be based on a formula – say, valuing the business at two times revenue. Don't use profit, because which non-exec team will discard you if you are delivering lots of profit?

Use two valuations to protect your share value

A non-exec team may decide that the business could generate more profit if you were out of the way.

If this is the case, then you'll be paid for the cancellation of your work contract and, ideally, you want to be able to sell your shares. A shareholder agreement which protects your interests will allow you to value your shares, on being asked to leave, using the best of two methods – either revenue or profit – and allowing you to choose the higher valuation. This way you are covered. If you are forced out when the business revenues are strong but profits are weak, your shares will use the revenue valuation. If the business growth has slowed down and profits are stable but strong, then your preferred measure will be profit.

Even so, a formulaic method of valuing your shares might not be a great deal for you; you should retain the right to go out to the marketplace to see if you can sell your shares for a higher price. But at the very least your contract should give you a clear exit with a minimum payout for your shares.

New investors may well pay more for your shares if the non-exec team is good and have made the right decision to let you go; then the prospects of the business will be stronger and new investors should be identifiable. If not, then the claim of the non-executives that you are rubbish and should leave is evidently somewhat weak. All you can do is put it down to their own weaknesses and move on.

98.

Cease trading before it is too late

If your business is going down hill rapidly, as will sometimes happen if a market collapses or you suffer a product failure, then it may be better to bail out sooner rather than later.

By bailing out, I mean to cease trading and then – and only then – to let an appointed liquidator make all staff (if you have any) redundant, and negotiate to escape from the terms of any contract (such as the rent of office space). Liquidators are simply specialist accountants and are usually from a sub-division of a larger accounting firm. Rather as some firms have specialist tax partners, others have specialist accountants who work specifically on liquidations.

Create a freelance skeleton staff before the business goes wrong

If the business still has diminished but still has reasonable prospects and can expect to meet its bills when they fall due, then reduce your staff to a team of entirely freelance or short-term contract workers and create a smaller re-focused team from your previous one to carry out the obligations required by the business.

For instance, you may have sold an annual subscription to your customers. In which case, you must either provide the remainder of that subscription or return the portion of the subscription that was unused.

In this case it may be better to continue on a skeleton basis rather than refund all the money. At least at the end of the year you will probably have a depleted but still valuable subscriber list and your brand will still be in tact.

Be careful here: You can't make staff redundant when you know the business is in trouble. Therefore, you must make them redundant beforehand. Once you believe that your business may not be able to meet its obligations (or pay its debts) when they fall due, then you must be careful not to prejudice one creditor (i.e. person or business to whom you owe money) above another. Hence, if you were to make a member of staff redundant and pay their redundancy, and a few weeks later you closed the business and left other people unpaid, then the unpaid creditors could sue you personally (no limited liability protection here).

This all adds up to yet another reason for changing to a freelance staffing structure and sticking to it! In a freelance staff structure, employment law and redundancy doesn't become an issue to derail your business – or, indeed, your own private finances and well-being.

Close down subsidiary businesses first (especially foreign ones)

If you have a UK company that also owns other businesses (limited companies or limited liability partnerships) in the UK or in other countries, then your main UK business is acting as a holding company (i.e. holding the shares and control of other businesses).

If you close the holding company before you shut the subsidiary companies, you'll have all sorts of trouble getting the necessary consents from the liquidator to close those subsidiaries.

And, if you have subsidiaries outside the mother company's country then you really are in trouble. Your liquidator will either not understand the company law in that country, or worse will understand – and will be charging exceptionally high rates for their expertise.

It is simple, close the subsidiaries first and then the holding company.

So, if you think that there is a risk that your holding company may cease trading, start to close your subsidiaries down quickly. It can take upwards of a year to cleanly close a business in Europe. Don't fall into the trap of delaying in the hope that the business might recover.

Understanding the types of liquidation

If you've never been through insolvency before, there is no reason why you would know much about it – but a basic working knowledge is a must for all entrepreneurs. This isn't pessimism but the kind of practical information that might just save your entrepreneurial career. The most successful business maverick in the world isn't that safe without it.

There are three types of insolvency:

1. The first is where you voluntarily cease trading and declare that the business can pay off the creditors with the cash and assets that remain when you cease trading (note: employees become creditors if their redundancy money is not fully covered by the government). In the UK this is called a Member Voluntary Liquidation (MVL).

2. The second is where you voluntarily cease trading and are not absolutely sure of being able to meet all creditors' payments (i.e. you are not willing or able to make a sworn statement to the fact that you can meet all creditors' payments). In the UK this is called a Creditors' Voluntary Liquidation (CVL).

3. The third is where your creditors force you to cease trading (i.e. it is not your choice) and you usually owe the creditors a large amount (or large percentage) of money. In the UK this is called a Compulsory Liquidation.

Beware that in the case of the CVL the liquidators have a deep conflict of interest. They will ask the directors to recommend their firm as the liquidator; however, this decision is dependent on the creditors, not the directors, and will be settled at the creditors' meeting.

Should the creditors suspect, fairly or otherwise, that the directors of the business have not acted in their best interests, then the creditors will want to appoint their own liquidator.

However, even if the directors manage to persuade the creditors to appoint their chosen liquidator, the liquidator is not working for the directors but for the creditors and may make a director's life hell simply so that he or she appears impartial.

Never forget, the insolvency practitioners have a duty of care primarily to the creditors – not to you, the director. Equally, whilst the liquidator may appear to kindly offer their services to the directors of a company discussing the merits of MVL versus CVL, they stand to earn much bigger fees in the case of a business which is not able to meet its creditors' payments directly (CVL), and hence are unlikely to advise directors to opt for MVL, regardless of the relative merits.

Therefore, as a director, you are unwise to rely on *any* advice from insolvency practitioners, and imprudent to believe that they are similar to a trusted accountant (even if recommended by your trusted accountant). This is not to say that there is any out-and-out deceit involved in their job, simply that you must not be confused as to who they are working for – it isn't you. Don't fall for this classic error, no matter how nice they are.

A director who is a shareholder is most vulnerable

In the case where there is a risk that some creditors may not be paid in full, if you are a director who is also a shareholder then you are vulnerable to attack. So prepare yourself.

If a creditor can show that you did not act in their best interest when it became clear that the business was in trouble, then you can be disqualified as a director (that is, prevented from working as a director or running a business for some years) and the creditor can claim their debt against you personally.

You have no protection against this.

If you have a limited company, this might be a surprise. That's right – if you can be shown to have acted in bad faith as far as the creditors are concerned (and you can debate this meaning endlessly) then you, the director, become responsible for the money owed to a creditor.

And creditors who employ tough lawyers will know to threaten you with this scenario simply to scare you into an agreement to benefit their clients, even if they think they won't win.

So, don't believe that as a director you are safe and protected by the limited liability of your company. You are not. Run your business accordingly.

Don't forget the things a director needs to do

If you have run your business for years and see your dream fade before you, you might be tempted to just chuck it all in and walk away. Don't.

Don't turn your back on a failing business, no matter how tempting.

As a director you need to make sure that you remain protected by the limited liability of the company or partnership and so:

- do not do anything to harm the rights of the creditors

- *do* put the business into insolvency (or cease trading) before it is too late or you are forced to do so (and, ideally, when there is enough money to pay the creditors)

- do not take out any *extra* fees, dividends or pay 12 months before the business ceases to trade, or you'll have to pay them back. Normal contractual fees or team members' pay are okay.

The 12-month rule of protection

The good news is that anything you did at least 12 months ago or earlier, before the date of ceasing to trade, cannot be considered as acting in bad faith by creditors. Hence, if you decide to take money out of one of your businesses, or pay yourself a large dividend, you must be sure that you can do this at least 12 months before you may be forced to cease trading.

Alternatively, simply be prepared to pay it back during the first 12 months, after which you can safely spend or invest it without risk.

Now, no insolvency practitioner on earth is going to tell you this – because they would be showing you how to work the rules to your advantage. Still, I'm not an insolvency practitioner and I'm not intending to become one either.

From hero to villain

Once a successful or established business declares that it is ceasing to trade, then the director/shareholder will turn from hero to villain. You will go from someone whose business everyone wanted to win, to the villain who lost them business or work.

It is important that you are prepared for this shift in sentiment. Or, if you are not prepared for it, that you at least realise that this is simply the way of human beings.

Do not take it personally, although many personal insults may be directed at you. This is simply people realising that they didn't make a lot of money out of you, and sometimes that just makes them a little green with envy.

Oddly, you may find that many people dislike seeing you walk away without obligation. Somehow there is a warped human logic that says that as the founder you should suffer.

Well, it is my advice that you should plan to lay low and keep your own counsel and be prepared to stay away from certain people until they have moved on in their own lives.

Just don't take it personally. It is, remember, not about you, but about how other people feel. And that is neither in your control, nor your responsibility.

Dead period between ceasing to trade and creditors' meeting

Very few people will tell you this, certainly not a liquidator, but there is a period of around two to four weeks between a company's decision to cease trading (called the beginning of the winding-up process) and the point where the responsibility for the business is passed to the liquidator, who will be appointed at the creditors' meeting (by the creditors – that is, not the previous directors).

During this time the liquidator, who has been proposed by the directors but has not yet been appointed, will write to all potential creditors to inform them of the company's decision and invite them, if they believe they are owed money, to submit a request, and provide them with the details of the creditors' meeting which they may attend (in person or via an elected person).

During this period, the business cannot pay any bills and no sales can be made that can't be immediately fulfilled (from stock, say). The directors are nominally in charge of the business, essentially to ensure that no one runs off with the assets, but without effective power.

The directors are not typically paid for this service if there are insufficient funds to meet the creditors' demands.

It is wise to plan for this period to be as short as possible and to ensure that everything is in order before the decision to cease trading is made. If you have assets, such as a valuable mailing list, this list will be at risk of theft or simply being deserted during this period.

What can go wrong at the creditors' meeting

The creditors' meeting is designed to review the sworn declarations of the directors, to ask questions about the management of the business in the previous 12 months and to appoint the liquidator.

However, creditors may vote to appoint their own liquidator, and not necessarily the liquidator proposed by the directors. A liquidator imposed by creditors will typically look favourably on the creditors and give the directors a tough time!

The decision on who becomes liquidator is put to a vote based on the amount owed. So, for each £1 each creditor is owed they get one vote. Directors may also be creditors and so have a vote. Whichever proposed liquidator receives the greatest number of votes wins.

Just don't lose this creditors' meeting vote – it is very important. Before you cease trading you need to calculate how many of the creditors you can keep on your side. This means speaking to all the creditors, especially the big ones, and telling them what is happening.

It is easy to do, and a classic mistake I made, to be so involved in trying to make the right decision about continuing or closing the business and what happens to your team that you forget to speak to the biggest creditors. Don't do this. Remember that big creditors will determine how the business gets wrapped up – swiftly and cleanly or with bitterness and recriminations.

Essentially, when a business is in trouble, your priority is no longer to satisfy shareholders or look after your team, but to take care of creditors.

Don't pay one creditor and not another

So, you won't be surprised to learn that prior to putting the business into liquidation the directors have a legal obligation to ensure that they have done nothing to prejudice creditors' interests. This is a legal requirement.

Simply put, you cannot pay one creditor and not another. Equally, you should sign no obligation (i.e. for a loan) if you believe the business is close to a decision to cease trading. Remember, if an employee is made redundant or is owed money, they become a creditor too.

Doctors with a good bedside manner don't get sued

Don't forget the critical insight revealed by Malcolm Gladwell in his book *Blink*: it is the doctors who communicate well with their client that don't get sued. Those doctors who don't take time to talk to their clients get sued more often, even if they are better doctors.

So, speak to your creditors. You need to work hard to keep them onside at this critical time.

99.

Choose the right opportunity

Ultimately, success as an entrepreneur comes from choosing the right opportunity. That way you don't have to be the brightest, you don't have to work the hardest, but you still do better than anyone else, simply because you chose the right opportunity.

So how do you know which is the right opportunity for you?

Begin… be willing to fail…follow your passion…and keep going.

Begin

Everybody has to begin somewhere – but too many would-be entrepreneurs never begin. They are too busy waiting to fund their idea to get started; they are too busy writing the spreadsheet business plan to kick-start the business. Throughout this book I've laid out rules to guide and help, but they are all worthless if you don't begin. And, no matter where you are, you will never have the perfect conditions, and you may not even have the right opportunity at the very beginning. Don't let that stop you.

Be willing to fail

Until you begin – in a real and practical way – to put your business idea into practice, you really cannot know if something is the right opportunity, but once you've begun, if you keep your eyes open, whether it is the right opportunity will become clear. You can only get to it, however, by being willing to fail.

I began my life as an entrepreneur working with health products – interesting and lucrative and I learnt a lot, but not where my passion lay. My next, and first fully fledged business was digital publishing – started back in 1999 when no one was making money selling eBooks or online information. We found – by trial and error and launching a range of eBooks, downloadable games and online tools – that what sold was books and software on property investment.

We used the real world as our test tube, launching aloe vera health books which sold weakly, murder mystery games of which we sold a couple, and then a complex online picture-driven goal system which flopped.

Slowly, we realised that we had a strong property investment publishing business.

So these things can be arrived at by degrees. But no one ever arrived at them by refusing to set out in the first place. And no one ever arrived at them by being overly scared of failure, either in the beginning or along the way.

Follow your passion

Lastly, make sure you are fulfilling your passion. I love publishing but over time the business I began as a digital publishing company in 1999 turned out to be a property-selling business. In hindsight, once I realised this shift it would have been better to have sold out and let someone passionate about property take it over. I actually ended up missing out on opportunities in publishing because I was clinging onto something I could no longer be passionate about.

So if you can combine these three – getting going, being fearless and making sure you remain passionate – then all that remains is for you to keep going.

Keep going

Clearly, you can expect to meet setbacks along the way. You will meet successes too. The key to turning the good and bad, the successes and disappointments, into a great entrepreneurial journey, is *you*. If you keep going, if you keep learning, if you keep trying out the next thing, then you will make it, one way or another.

And, to help do this, always remember that you are bigger than any single business or business opportunity, which is my next and final rule...

100.

Business comes, business goes – you'll always be an entrepreneur

Entrepreneurs identify very closely with their businesses and brands. This is a good thing at the time, but later you have to break away – preferably with cash in hand, ideas in mind and time to spare. Sometimes it'll be your own choice, and other times, regrettably, it'll be the choice of others.

But however you leave, never forget that you are an entrepreneur, and that is someone who starts business*es* – and that's a plural.

You are not the business and the business is not you. There are times to let it go – in good and bad circumstances – and move on with your entrepreneurial work. You are always bigger than the business; much, much bigger.

Becoming great at being an entrepreneur is not a short journey; just as developing a special skill in any field, it takes time, dedication and passion. However, the one thing that seems to set long-term successful entrepreneurs apart from those that fall by the wayside is that successful entrepreneurs learn to deal with disappointment or failure. As said, I learnt more in my last two years watching my previous business fall apart than I did in the previous eight years of rapid growth.

Every business that innovates will experience failure – just as Thomas Edison experienced failure many times in his search for the electric light bulb, or J. K. Rowling had her manuscript for the first Harry Potter book rejected by numerous publishers. Behind almost every success, in business and in life, there lies a series of disappointments. If you ever have to wonder if you can do it, or do it again, the answer of thousands who have gone before you is an emphatic *yes*.

Postscript

Much of the advice I have given in this book is not especially politically correct; and some people will say that these Rules, particularly in regards to staff, are overly harsh. You are free to judge this for yourself.

In my experience, harshness is a matter of *how* you implement, not *what* you implement.

My experience has taught me that not taking tough action quickly usually only delays and magnifies the seriousness of steps you have to take later on. Hence, no one really benefits in the long run from being 'nice' by avoiding necessary action. And, remember, hard decisions don't have to be delivered harshly.

If you hold exceptionally high standards and are able to implement actions (both easy and tough) to maintain those standards, then you can be seen as a caring manager but, more importantly, as a great person to work with and for.

You are going to make mistakes. It is all a part of growing as an entrepreneur. It is natural to be concerned about mistakes and to do everything you can to avoid them. Hopefully this book has helped you by guiding you around the biggest errors, or at least left you able to recognise them if you *have* made them, and shown you how to avoid them next time round. Of course, you'll find that some of the ideas in this book conflict when applied to your sector or to your business idea. In such cases, you'll need to decide which to prioritise and which to drop or ignore. Most of what entrepreneurs do is a mix of learning the theory and applying and refining it through trial and error. Each entrepreneur has a slightly different style and may go about things in a different way, but ultimately many of the principles are the same.

If this book can add three years to your learning and maturing process as an entrepreneur, then it will be worth its weight in gold, even if it can't instantly guarantee you immediate success and riches. (No one can, of course; be wary of those who say otherwise.)

I'm always developing and sharing my thoughts about what makes a great entrepreneur and what we can learn from others who have trod what is the most unique, challenging and rewarding path in business. If you'd like to hear more, please join the free newsletter at **www.RagstoWreckages.com**.

Neil